and
Teaching
Black Young Adults

An Exposition toward Strengthening the Church through Ministry to Urban Black Young Adults

Rev. Walter Arthur McCray

Black Light Fellowship

2859 W. WILCOX ST. • CHICAGO, IL 60612
POST OFFICE BOX 5369 • CHICAGO, IL 60680
PUBLICATIONS

(312) 722-1441

Publisher

Black Light Fellowship
*2859 W. WILCOX ST. * CHICAGO, IL 60612*
*POST OFFICE BOX 5369 * CHICAGO, IL 60680*

(312) 722-1441

ISBN: 0-933176-07-4

LC # 86-71996

Scripture quotations are from the *Authorized Version*
(KJV) unless otherwise noted. The following abbrevia-
tions are used: TEV, *Today's English Version;* RSV,
Revised Standard Version; NKJV, *New King James
Version;* NIV, *New International Version.*

Printed in the United States of America

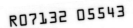
*To all Black Christian leaders
who have committed themselves
to the ministry of
assisting Black adolescents
emerge into Christ-centered
Black young adult men and women.*

Reaching and Teaching Black Young Adults
Rev. Walter Arthur McCray

Contents

Foreword

One of the greatest needs of Black Congregations in the Christian community is for dedicated teachers of the Bible who possess the literary talent and expertise to competently express in writing their thoughts with journalistic skills.

Much of the literature and books of the Church do not adequately meet the varied ministries of our congregations; because they were not written within the context of the unique Black spiritual experiences that is characteristic of our communities of faith.

It is therefore most refreshing to have the Lord raise up from our ranks a Reverend Walter Arthur McCray, whose insights and understanding of the Word not only reflect such experiences, but significantly impact our Fellowships with explanations of the Word that are doctrinally sound and spiritually edifying.

Reaching and Teaching Black Young Adults is one such exposition. Its message carries promise for many years to come.

Reverend Arthur D. Griffin, Th.D.
First Baptist Congregational Church
Chicago, IL

Preface

In the midst of performing editing responsibilities and meeting deadlines for two quarterly productions, one would imagine how there could be found any space in such a crowded schedule for writing a book and preparing it for publication. Yet, when the need became manifest, we "took our pen in hand" and somehow managed to get the manuscript finished on time, rushing to press with the final product.

The idea for an instructional resource for teachers of Black young adults was broached by Melvin E. Banks, President of Urban Ministries, Inc./Urban Outreach. The resource was meant to complement the organizations' new Sunday School literature, **Young Adult TODAY.** We immediately recognized the need of the wider Black Christian community for such a treatment.

As I began preparing this work, I was moved with a sense of gratitude for the *National Black Christian Students Conference.* My knowledge and experience working with young adults has been greatly enriched as a result of participating in and serving the *Conference* for over 12 years. Our ministry of planning quality and relevant programs, for Black Christian young adult college and graduate students and for community leaders, has well-suited me to approach this subject. The *Conference* has contributed significantly to my understanding of what kind of ministry can best help Black young men and women, developing their leadership potential for the Black Church and community.

Reaching and Teaching Black Young Adults contains more than the eye initially captures. For interwoven through this work is a theological and spiritual concept for assisting

the wholistic development of Black American young adults —
an extremely important age group — through a process of
maturation referred to as "emergence." Of sorts, this work
encapsulates the goal of a "rights of passage" for Black young
adults, and reveals successive steps to be attained on the
way.

Perhaps the reader can get a better grasp of my feelings
about this work by my relating two simple thoughts that
occurred to me while writing. First, we were brought into a
realization of how crucial this study is when we began grap-
pling with the issue, *Who is a Black **young adult?*** The answer
to this question was not readily apparent, as evidenced by the
differences of opinion among educators and the varied grada-
tions used among Christian circles. We considered it a challenge to formulate a meaningful basis for distinguishing those
we call "young adults" from "teens" on the one side and from
"adults" on the other. At the least, the discussion proved
invigorating.

Second, following close behind the former discussion, we
were pressed with providing a criteria by which the emergence
of a Black young person into full young adulthood could be
reasonably measured. This process was downright exciting
and enlightening. We came forth was a set of criteria (nine
points in all) which we think are really essential and can stand
the test. In the midst of writing I thought to myself that it
would have been good for me to have had this criteria when I
was about 17 or 18. These standards would have been most
helpful to my personal and social maturation during my own
journey across the stage of Black young adulthood. Perhaps
the message on these pages will spare many adolescents the
troubles of life caused by lack of direction during this important phase of human, social and spiritual development.

Those leaders who serve urban Black young adults, Christian or otherwise, should find this educational resource both

an enlightening and provocative publication. It continues the modest tradition of **Black Light Fellowship** which seeks to provide Christ-centered Black Christian literature for members of the Black Christian community.

Not to be forgotten, we owe a gracious word of thanks to several helpful individuals for their assistance in this project: to *Rosita E. McClain*, our secretary, for taking care of many details, and, *especially*, for checking each Scripture and reference; to *Ronald E. Maney*, our dedicated artist, for his good and gracious service in providing the cover art-work; to *Melvin E. Banks* for his editorial analysis; to *Jawanza Kunjufu*, our brother in the Lord, in the struggle, and in writing, for a few informative and reflective hours; to my pastor, *Arthur D. Griffin*, for his encouragement and assistance; and to *First Baptist Congregational Church*, for being supportive of this publication venture. A special gratitude is owed **Thelma** *my wife* for her prayers and for absorbing the many responsibilities she always does when I retreat into my writing hole. And for those persons whose names remain unwritten, but whose willingness to assist, prayers and moral support has been evidenced, we say "much thanks!"

Without the wisdom and strength of the Lord, this project would not have run its course. It is He alone Who is deserving of my worship.

REACHING AND TEACHING BLACK YOUNG ADULTS

First Part

Understanding Black Young Adults

Introduction

Without question, the greatest potential of the Black Church today resides in the group we call "young adults."

Those persons in this group are no longer teens or "young people," and they have yet to reach full adulthood. Nevertheless, this particular, though in some ways amorphous, age-group, either through their meaningful and responsible participation or lack of it, will determine the qualitative development of the churches and communities of Black Americans into the twenty-first century.

Young adults are an important group to the Church, and their influential presence is increasingly coming to bear upon our churches and their traditional ways. Thus, it is to this age group that Black Christian pastors, parents, educators, and youth workers must quickly turn their attention in order to properly address the needs and oversee the growth of Black young adults into full maturity. For the sacred trust of the Christian faith — the faith of Jesus Christ — sooner or later will pass within their purview. And as it does, their manner of handling this sacred trust will become the telltale sign indicating whether their leaders have effectively taught and brought them into complete maturation, and whether they have spiritually prepared these emerging young men and women to fulfill the Christian charge both in their churches and in their generation.

But specifically, who are these emerging Black young adults, and how does one recognize them when he sees them?

Without hesitation, the question of understanding Black young adults precedes the questions of how best to reach and to teach them. If we do not understand Black young adults — that is, who they are, the scope of their age range, their predominant characteristics, their needs and their desires, their manner of thinking and living, etc. — we will fail to reach them. And those whom we have already reached, we will fail to adequately teach. So, at the outset, it is essential and of first importance that we take a fresh and careful look at this human/social developmental stage of life for the purpose of gaining a good understanding of young adult men and women.

Chapter 1

Identifying Black Young Adults

Introduction

The question was put to a Black pastor, "What is a Black young adult?" His reply, "A Black young adult is a Black adult who is young!"

Beneath this touch of humor lies an obvious truth. If the question of what composes Black **adulthood** is clearly answered, then the question of Black **young** adulthood follows in its tracts. However, the question of Black adulthood, though most of us would assume a common physiological understanding, is not so simple to answer. And its answer is predicated on first identifying Black manhood and Black womanhood in the American context.

Though impacting this work, these wider identifications would be better dealt with in separate treatments. In this work we limit ourselves to addressing Black young adulthood. In doing so we remember that many of us hold diverse and sometimes contrary understandings of Black adulthood, manhood and womanhood. The author, like other educators, does have a concept of what constitutes Black American adulthood, including both its male and female components. And implications of these views should become apparent as this work progresses. With this in mind, the message of these pages should not be viewed in isolation from the wider Black American adult experience.

So, our first task in this discussion is to arrive at a good working definition of Black young adults. The factors which inform this definition are multi-dimensional.

A. Classified by their Age-Range

If we start from the lower end of the age scale, the task of identifying Black young adults is made quite simple. Following are the three basic periods of life with suggested age ranges: childhood (birth-13), adolescence (13-17), and adulthood (18+).

If we follow this pattern, young adults would be those persons at the lower end of the adult period. Thus, Black young adults are those persons who no longer are in the age-group which characterizes those who have graduated the public high school system (provided they have successfully kept pace with their required course of study.) That is, young adulthood commences around 17 or 18 years of age. Now it is at this point that the simplicity of defining Black young adulthood ceases.

For instance, at what age point do we separate Black young adults from adults? A sampling of the opinions of several persons who work with post adolescents is quite revealing.

One associate (Ruth Bentley, Ph.D., a Black psychologist and Chairperson of the National Black Christian Students Conference, who has been working with Black young adults for over two decades) says that the cut off point is around thirty-three. Another associate (Ronald Maney, a graduate student concentrating on the relationship of the Black male to the Black Church and working in a family counseling center) says the determining age is around twenty-seven.

A senior pastoral friend says the age cut-off for young adults is about forty-five years! However, he sees young adulthood beginning, not at age 17 or 18 but, around twenty-five years. One colleague in his late twenties says that for a young adult in his church not to be considered an adult at age twenty-four would be rather insulting. And then there are those who,

15

based on the climate of the '60's, would hold that age 30 is the high-water mark.

The authors of *Understanding People* (Evangelical Teacher Training Association, pg. 75) give the following division: *later adolescence or young adulthood, 18-34; middle adulthood, 35-64; older adulthood, 65+.*

Though there are certain objective factors which must be included in any worthy identification of young adulthood, it nevertheless remains the case that concretely identifying young adults becomes a matter of who is doing the identifying and for what purpose the identification is being used.

At this point a critical question is raised: What criteria is used to arrive at any particular age cut-off point, thus lessening or removing arbitrariness from any given identification of young adulthood? The following should provide us with some guidelines that will help us identify those we call "young adults."

B. Characterized by their Emergence

Black young adults are **a group in emergence.** Their emerging can be viewed from two perspectives, where they are coming from and where they are going.

If for working purposes we accept the following age divisions, we will be better able to see the emerging character of young adulthood. (It may be helpful to note that in different Church, denominational and Christian educational circles sometimes different terminology is used to refer to the same age group. For example, one person may use the term "young people" in reference to younger adolescents (13-16), while another may use the identical term in reference to those who have graduated high school (17-20).)

Following the pattern of Jawanza Kunjufu (author of *Countering the Conspiracy to Destroy Black Boys*, Afro-Am, 1983) we can make the following three-fold age-division on the lower side of young adulthood: *children, infants-9; youth, 9-13; and young people (teens, adolescents), 13-18.* Then if we modify the adult categories previously mentioned, we also have a three-fold age-division on the higher side of young adulthood: *early adult, 19-34; middle adult, 35-64; and older adult, 65+.*

Now the period we are targeting as "young adulthood" would fall between the two three-fold age groupings. And it overlaps one period from each group, spanning from 17 on the lower side to 24 on the higher side. Thus, we have the following:

Children - Youth - Young People (teens, adolescents)
(Infant-9)   (9-13)   (13-16——18)

- YOUNG ADULT -
(17-24)

Early Adult - Middle Adult - Older Adult
(19——25-34)   (35-64)   (65+)

Based, then, on these divisions we are able to pinpoint young adults. Keeping in mind that some understand young adulthood extending up through age 35, we choose to identify (for all practical working purposes) the period of young adulthood as covering ages 17-24. This is the age-span on which we should focus our concentration if we are to adequately understand and minister to this important group. As we shall discuss later, it is our belief that by the age of 23 or 24 the Black young adult should have completed his full maturation into this phase of life, and from that point on (up through age 35) he should be preparing himself/herself for settling into complete adulthood.

Our reason for classifying young adults as we do is based on our understanding of the maturational process they are undergoing. Black young adults are emerging from late adolescence and they are emerging into full adulthood. They are experiencing a gradual socialization process during a most critical season of human social development.

Black young adults are in transition from childhood into adulthood, from depending on others for survival to depending on self for survival. They are in a state of change and intensification that differs from the roller-coaster experience of many adolescents. And they are settling but not established like most middle adults. Black young adults are emerging in that they are "rising up and coming forth" into maturity, and into the wholeness which we characterize as adulthood. In short, they are "coming into their own."

"Emerging" appears to be the best terminological basis from which to tie-together a composite concept of Black young adulthood. This terminology can help us to arrive at a general working definition of this important group to whom the Church must address herself if she is to further her growth and development.*

(In most cases throughout this work we will attempt to follow the procedure of trying to keep the writing style smooth and unencumbered. So, unless otherwise stated or understood, "he/his/him" is used generically and includes male and female; "parents" is used ideally but a single "parent" or a "guardian" may better suit the case, and be more in line with prevailing social conditions.)

C. Recognized by varied Signs of Maturity

There appear to be several factors which observers of young people note as signs indicating a young person is becoming a young adult.

1. Economically

Economically, there is a move away from parental dependency toward independence. This move should not be mistaken for the move made by many Black young people away from their family/parent support-group to their peers, e.g. into gangs. The teen-age peer group provides emotional, psychological and social support. But the burden of the financial support comes via the parents to the young person.

A young person is recognized as becoming a young adult when he begins to take an active responsibility in his own economic survival. No longer are the parents regarded as the primary economic providers. The parents may offer assistance or emergency help, but the young person looks to himself for providing his own economic base.

This economic base provided by the young person for himself will support his place to stay, food to eat, utilities, spouse and/or children, transportation, church offerings, recreational activities, continued education, etc. This will be accomplished through some means of gainful employment, though other means of reaching financial independence may not be excluded, e.g. public assistance.

2. Psychologically

Psychologically, the young person begins to define himself as a young adult and sets-out to live accordingly. This is a definite sign of maturity.

Somewhere in the phase between the late teen years and the early 20's the young person makes a conscious choice in the area of self-identification. He looks at himself and his life differently. In no uncertain terms will he allow others to continue classing or placing him among young people. He is now different and wants to be related to differently.

The other side of this coin finds the new young adult (self-identified) changing his associations and movements. He begins to move in older circles, and frequents activities and places where young adults can be found. Sometimes his behavior shifts back toward the teens, yet his sights are becoming fixed. He is aware and sensitive to young adulthood. He is feeling his way, but likes what he is experiencing. He is a young adult and wants to be one fully.

3. Socially

Socially, there is the recognition and affirmation by a representative cross-section of the older adults in the community that the young person is an adult. The community here is used of the wider circle in which the young person moves outside his peer-group. It includes both parents and other adults.

The parents play an important part in the social perception of the emergent young adult. For instance, how the young person is portrayed by the parents over the phone and to the neighbors is a factor. And how the young person is treated by the parents in the presence of older adults in the neighborhood or at church is another factor. As the parents give a new status to their young person, so will other adults tend to follow suit.

And the children of the community will follow suit as well. For according to the lead and instruction of the parents and

19

the other adults in the community, the children will be required and begin to refer to the emergent young adult as "Mr." or "Ms." so and so. The children will begin relating to the emergent young adult as an adult.

Older adults with whom the young person comes into association also play a part in the social perception of the emerging young adult. These adults may be co-workers of the young person observing how he handles the work-a-day world. They may be teachers and counselors at church observing spiritual growth. They may be watchful neighbors observing the young person's natural behavior with children or those of the opposite sex, which behavior sends signals of immaturity or maturity.

The age of the young person relative to the age-span of those in one's community, young as well as old, may affect how the community perceives an individual. If there are not many youth or adolescents in a community, the young person may at a sooner age be regarded as a young adult. If there are many young people in the community and also many middle-aged adults, the young person may not be regarded as a young adult quite as soon.

When the parent of the young person and other significant adults in his life instinctively feel and perceive a change in the young person toward adulthood, they will begin to relate to him as an adult. In so doing, the community will reinforce the self-identification which the emerging young adult has placed on himself.

4. Accountability-wise

Accountability-wise, the emergent young adult is becoming totally responsible for making his own decisions, and for establishing his own actions and behavior. In this regard, one day he will become socially/legally in subjection to no other.

Just as the parents of the man born blind related to the Pharisees concerning their own son, so the emergent young adult is "of age." Of his own right he is able to speak for himself. Legally, the young person is not bound by his parents, for instance, to continue attending school. If he commits a crime the authorities do not come searching for his parents, but for him. He votes for himself, he may enlist in the Arm

Services for himself, he can enter into business dealings by himself, and he can sign his own self into or out of the hospital.

He is legally free, but he is also held accountable by the society for his own decisions and his actions. If his business deal turns sour, he must suffer the consequences. If he needs car insurance, he must establish his own insurability with an insurance corporation. And if he doesn't make a wise choice, his parents are not responsible for restoring his wrecked car or for paying the hospital bill of an injured party because their son was underinsured. If he enters a promotional contest and wins, he can collect the prize in full, for he is no longer a minor.

5. Emotionally

Related to the above, emotionally, the emergent young adult is prepared to accept the full consequences for his own decisions and actions. He has no one to blame or to praise but himself.

If the financial dealings of the young person blossom into prosperity, he can enjoy his success to the hilt. But if his momentous plans fail to pan-out, he must be prepared to accept failure, critique himself, pick up the pieces and get on with life.

The emergent young adult grows to accept the reality of the strains and tensions associated with the decision-making processes. There is no one who will wisely step into the realm where the young person turning young adult mentally and emotionally surrenders to an unbearable dilemma. The emergent young adult cannot default in making decisions, and still respectfully claim young adulthood. And what further shock awaits him if he allows some other person to make choices for him which he must live with for the rest of his life! This is especially so when the adviser/decider begins to withdraw from the young adult's situation and says, "Don't blame me for your trouble, I was only trying to help you!"

The young person turning young adult becomes emotionally mature and responsible.

6. Value-wise

Value-wise, most young adults have affectively and reasonably determined their values and are following a course of life that is accordant with them. There is a settling of the emergent young adult's belief system. By contrast, adolescents are experimenting with their values and searching for a place to land.

Young adults are becoming less tentative about life, which experience is fast clearing and moving before their eyes. They realize that if they are going to succeed in life they must "go for it." If they value education or what education can bring, they proceed through undergraduate and graduate school. If they are career oriented, they move into opportune openings, orient, and situate themselves to move ahead. If they value the things of the Lord, they become responsibly and more actively involved in the work of the Church. If they desire a marriage they will pursue those relationships which carry potential for serious development. If "money is the name of the game," everything the emergent young adult does will lead toward this end.

Whether one agrees or disagrees with the value-choices of an emergent young adult, one thing is unmistakable: they pursue what they believe is right for them be and to have.

7. Community-wise

Community-wise, there is an evident responsibleness exercised in the community by the emergent young adult. With a "taken-for-granted" attitude, the adolescent survives on the resources of the community. In contrast, the emergent young adult shares in the development of the community.

Though it is readily admitted that this criteria for recognizing the emergent young adult in a "me-istic," "individualistic" generation is not applicable to all, yet it still can be used to recognize some. A genuine young adult is a community-responsible young adult. He is consciously aware of being an asset in his neighborhood.

Others in the community begin to recognize the young-adultness of a person when he begins to make significant contributions to his community. He may assume a leadership role, especially in relation to the younger members of the community. He may also become actively involved in a block club, political organization, cultural center, or some other social service endeavor. In short, his social visibility increases in a more or less community-helper role.

The emergent young adult is no longer satisfied with only watching things happen around him. Instead he wants to participate in making things happen and in shaping their outcome. And when the adults of the community recognize this aspect of maturity in a young adult, they will usually make it possible for such an one to be placed in a position of responsibility that requires a degree of trustworthiness. They will become comfortable working with and functioning under the leadership of the community-responsible young adult.

Succinctly, a sign of maturity of the emergent young adult is the concern he has for giving himself to the development of other persons. Having himself become in a measure secure with reaching his own development at a given stage of life, the emergent young adult gives of himself to help others.

8. Volitionally *(according to the will)*

Volitionally, the emergent young adult voluntarily submits himself to a process of growing. Willingly, and motivated intrinsically, he cooperates with the factors and dynamics that he believes will bring about his own maturational development.

The emergent Black young adult is one who has progressed beyond the stage where he must be forced to do what others believe will contribute to his overall well-being. So also, the emergent young adult has come to resist the tendencies to exploit his new freedoms (as his own primary decision-maker) into involving himself in only the pleasurable things of life. Instead, the young person who is becoming a young adult has brought himself to size up life and his experience (sometimes painfully), forces himself to "take charge" of his own growth (not just of his own lifestyle), and subjects himself to an appreciation of and the disciplines of growth.

In other words, the emergent young adult commits himself to a process of emergence. Oftentimes this factor of young adult development goes unnoticed. Yet its presence penetrates the young adult experience. One need only listen to the "growth-talk" present in the conversation of young adults. The careful listener will perceive a certain self-consciousness possessed by the young adult, of not only his person, but also of how different experiences are affecting his growth. He sort of acquires the ability to perceive himself from the outside. And on the basis of direction gained from weighing information from this self-awareness, the emergent young adult deliberately exercises his will to follow that direction.

A distinct though sometimes silent affirmation of the emergent young adult is: "I will grow; I will mature; I will become." And his conduct is made to follow suit by his emboldened and strengthened powers of the will.

9. Spiritually

Spiritually, the emergent young adult reaches a full assurance in the faith as a believer in the Lord Christ Jesus. Among other spiritual characteristics of this age-group, this aspect appears to be the one most telling, and does serve to comprehend the others. If the emergent young adult is one who is "coming into his own," the emergent young adult Christian is one who is **"coming into his own in the Lord."**

Though His age at the time fell short of our classification as a young adult, the experience of Jesus seems nevertheless an apropos model for the emergent young adult. After all, it was at the age of 12 that Jewish males traveled through their "rights of passage" into full manhood. The author cannot resist recalling the words of our Savior to his apprehensive parents when they returned to find Him in the temple of Jerusalem, teaching the elders. Jesus said to his parents: "Why is it that you sought Me? Did you not know that I must be about my Father's business?" (Luke 2:49, NKJV).

Surely this response of Jesus manifested His forthright emergence into "young adulthood." In affirmation of this thought, a study of the verses immediately following our Savior's words will reveal His progressive and wholistic growth toward the end of what can only be appropriately described as full adulthood (Luke 2:50-52).

Considered spiritually, the emergent Black young adult is

one who possesses what the Scripture calls a "full assurance of faith" (Hebrews 10:22; cf. 6:11; Colossians 2:2; 1 Thessalonians 1:5). Other synonymous phrases of the underlying Greek word (PLEROPHORIA) would include "entire confidence," and "full conviction." It is this quality of faith that becomes evident in the life of the emergent young adult. This full assurance of faith will be reflected in the young adult's personal relationship with Christ, in his understanding of God's will, in his wholistic maturity, and in his active and strong service for Christ and his own people. In actuality the full assurance of faith of the emergent Christian Black young adult affects all the other eight areas of his maturational development. We will further elaborate on these ideas throughout the balance of these pages.

At this point we will suffice to say that the Christian adolescent more or less believes what he has been taught. And it is the exception rather than the rule that a Christian young person spiritually increases more than his teachers. In contrast, the emergent Christian young adult, through the process of "sounding out" his convictions, comes to believe what he has examined and tried for himself. His faith in the Lord deepens appreciably, and his life is driven by a renewed spiritual authority. And if his leaders become lax, the emergent Christian young adult, both in learning and in living, is likely to leave those leaders "eating the dust."

With the full assurance of faith, the emergent Christian young adult is coming into his own in the Lord.

Summary

These foregoing are nine factors generally applicable to Black young adulthood. By them the emergent Black young adult is perceived economically, psychologically, socially, accountability-wise, emotionally, value-wise, and community-wise, volitionally, and spiritually.

There may be other factors useful for recognizing the emergent Black young adult, and carrying weight for other educators, that are not covered here. And the ones we have covered may receive greater or lesser importance to a given individual as the circumstances and need may require. However, these several sign-posts of recognition seem to be essential for perceiving emergent young adulthood as a whole and for measuring its progress.

Chapter 2

Profiling Black Young Adults

Introduction

At this point we can turn our attention toward observing young adults. We see them, but we need to know and feel them as they are from different dimensions.

Following are several glimpses of Black young adults who can be viewed culturally, socially, economically, psychologically, sexually, and spiritually. For the most part we concentrate on those who are between the ages 17 and 24.

When studying the life situation of Black young adults one thing should be kept in mind. Black young adults experience in their own way and at their own level that full range of experience known to all Black Americans. In many ways the experiences of the overwhelming majority of Black people in America are common to the group. Black young adults are no exception. What Black people are undergoing nationally, individual Black young adults are undergoing personally. Their experiences are a reflection of their people's experience.

A. Culturally

1. *There is Latrice.* She doesn't know Black history. She

typifies many Black young adults inasmuch as, relative to their parents and grandparents, they know little about the historical Black American experience. This would be more true for Black young adults in the northern part of the country than of those in the south, where Black history is taught as a matter of course in the public schools.

The tragedy is that Latrice is reaping the benefits of the civil rights and social revolution which took place in the 60's but doesn't realize it. She is totally unaware of many of the Black leaders of this era, and the contributions and sacrifices they made for the progress of Blacks during this time.

2. *There is Fred.* He is into the street. He has been into the streets ever since he dropped out of high school. Fred's world is a world of street-corners, basketball courts, pool-halls, cut-rate liquor stores, drugs, and some crime. He sleeps at home, but is in the street everyday. Fred is emotionally hard and he hustles for his money. He has previous gang experience but has outgrown the gang life, leaving it for the younger boys. Fred's culture is the street, and everything in it.

B. Socially

1. *There is Bobby.* He will be dead before he reaches 24. He has gone from one part-time job to another. He never has been caught up in any major trouble, only a few minor brushes with the law. He sort of lives on the fringes of the street. He can live with it or live without it. Generally Bobby is okay. But one day he will be caught in the wrong place at the wrong time. His life will be over before it even gets going good.

2. *There is Rita.* She is an unwed mother of two young children. Her life is centered around her children. She didn't finish high school but did earn her G.E.D. Rita stays at home with her mother and two younger sisters. Both of them receive food stamps and public assistance for their primary income. Most of her days are filled with T.V. "stories." When both her children get school-age she is determined to get herself some kind of job.

3. *There is Thomas.* He's the unwed father of three children by two different mothers. He doesn't live with either of the

mothers of his children. He does have a job, but it only pays a little above the minimum wage. He tries to give his children something every payday, but its not enough to go around. He loves his children but can't fully support them. Thomas spends a lot of time stroking his car, and is developing a drinking problem.

4. There is John. He graduated high school but doesn't know if he wants to go to college. He can fix cars and does some repair work from a friend's garage. John is not a good reader, and in some ways he is unsure of himself. He would be satisfied if he could get a mechanics job working for the city. That would be good money. But he still thinks about going to college, at least some junior college.

5. There is Ricky. He just finished his time in prison. He spent three years time because he and some of his partners got into a fight with some other dudes and he cut one. And the car they were driving when the police stopped them was stolen. Being in prison was some experience for Ricky — gangs, drugs, riots, homosexuality, exploitation by the guards, etc. Never in his life does he want to be locked behind bars again. Ricky has to report to his parole officer every week. He is trying to readjust to being back on the outside, and is desperately looking for a job so he can stay out of trouble.

C. Economically

1. There is Jerry. He is unemployed and 25. Believe it or not, never in his life has he ever held a full time job. Only part-time. Jerry really doesn't have a good skill on which to build. He didn't have a chance to consistently develop his potential. Jerry lives at home with his mother who at least provides a place for him to stay and some food to eat. He helps out around the house. He hangs out around the cab stand. If he can ever get his hands on enough money, he is going to get a ride so he can work the cab stand and the grocery store.

2. There is Betty. She is on public assistance. She can't do much because she is waaaaay over weight. Though she is only 28, she has a son who is into his third year in high school. Betty is able to work with her hands and likes to volunteer her services, but her weight is a problem. She gets a little extra money and some clothes and furniture by helping out at the resale shop every week. Betty stays in a small apartment with her sister who has four children of her own. Betty is counting on her son to finish high school and take care of his mama.

3. There is Catherine. She makes $37,000 a year. She is a court reporter with two-and-a-half years of college to her credit. She got the job through a tip from a friend who does para-legal work. Catherine considers her work the best thing going. She rents a high-rise apartment close to her city's business district. Designer clothes are her style. She eats out at least four nights a week. Catherine has a lot of free time on her hands which she uses to more or less "live it up." She likes to take long vacations during the summer. She comes from a small rural town but loves the city.

D. Psychologically

1. There is Tony. He has a chemical dependency. His problem is with drugs. He has been through three programs, but they have worked only for a while. Somehow Tony manages to keep a job, though several times he has come close to being dumped. Tony knows his habit is expensive and is ruining his life, but he likes it. Besides, he is hurting no one but himself.

2. There is Barbara. She is running from her Blackness. Somehow Barbara wishes that she weren't Black. Most of her close friends are white and they accept her as one of them, at least most of the time. Barbara seems like a misfit in the Black community. For some reason she doesn't feel like she is really accepted by her own people. She knows she is different, but believes that everybody should live in harmony. Barbara likes to work and move in integrated circles. Presently, she is working on developing a relationship she has with a white young man who has shown an interest in her. Barbara doesn't say much about her immediate family or early home-life. She sort of feels ashamed.

3. There is Alice. She is suicidal. Life seems too hard for her.

She is especially disappointed that she has not been able to develop a significant inter-personal relationship with any man. Is she lesbian? Alice has a good job and is success oriented. But neither seems to fully satisfy her life. "Isn't there more to life than I am getting?" "What's wrong with me?" she asks. There is a counselor Alice goes to see when she gets really depressed. But she has never really told her counselor what happened to her at home when she was six years old. If that ever gets out, she knows it will ruin her character reputation. Why does she have to be so miserable?

4. *There is Carl.* He seems to have it all together. Last year he graduated college. Immediately he was hired by the company that had hired him during his summer vacations. Carl is engaged to a beautiful sister. Their wedding is scheduled to take place in a few months. Carl already has a nice home and a good looking car. He is kind and genuinely concerned about other people. And whatever is happening, Carl seems to know something about it. Carl gets a lot of support from his parents. But it doesn't seem like he really needs it. He makes it on his own.

E. Sexually

1. *There is Wilfred.* He is gay. He has been gay for over twelve years, but has only come out of the closet in the last four or five years. His sexual preference is for young boys. Over the past several years Wilfred has worked his way through many of the hangups associated with the lifestyle he has chosen. Though at times he feels guilty, he does not show much shame about himself. The "gay rights" movement has opened him up. Wilfred works in youth programs.

2. *There is Anita.* She is sexually aggressive. Her appearance is most sensual and attractive, provocative clothing and all the rest. Anita prides herself in being "the new woman" and knows she has what it takes to satisfy a man. Though Anita is not as loose with her love-life as one might expect, she does have the reputation of having been involved in a significant number of passionate love affairs. Anita likes sex, and shows it.

3. *There is Milton.* He believes in sex "just like every other

man." He doesn't flaunt his activities, however sex is a routine part of who he is. Lately, Milton has been taking a closer look at his sexual involvements. AIDS is the problem. In no way does he want to contract the disease. He has become more selective of his sleeping companions.

4. *There is Sheila.* She is a newly wed and feels much relief in her new status. She is hoping for many years of marriage and complete uninhibited full sexual satisfaction from her husband. However, Sheila and her husband are encountering some sexual difficulties and she feels they need to make some adjustments. The problem is that Sheila is the only one willing to talk about it. Her husband doesn't talk about sex very much. The situation is becoming frustrating.

5. *There is Dave.* Believe it or not, Dave is a virgin. He did not make a conscious choice to follow this course, but this is the way his life is turning out. Dave spends a lot of time working with his mind. He reads a lot, and works with computers. He is studying to be an accountant. Dave does not appear to have any particular sexual hangups. His relationship with females appears normal. Sexual activity has never really been on his agenda. His interests are in other places.

F. Spiritually

1. *There is Rose.* She is actively involved in her church and loves the Lord Jesus. She is the divorced mother of one child, and struggling to please the Lord. Rose knows it is wrong for her to be sexually active as an unwed Christian, but feels she has no good alternative. She sings in the choir and tries to attend most of the church's activities. Rose reads her Bible and wants to become a Sunday School teacher.

2. *There is Joshua.* He is doing his best to work his way back into the church. He realizes that he needs the Lord, but doesn't want to be a hypocrite. He knows that some of the things that he is into are wrong. But the more he comes to church, the better he feels and the more he understands. Joshua knows he is going in the right direction. He likes the men's fellowship group at church. The older men make him feel welcomed, even though in some ways they are out of step with what is happen-

ing in the world. Then again, in some ways they really do know what is going on.

3. There is Kim. Kim grew up in the Church. Both her mother and father were church members and raised their family accordingly. Kim is dedicated to the Lord and her Church. Her personality is wholesome and her priorities, as best as she can determine, are all Christ-centered. Kim is a Bible believing and praying young woman. Every chance she gets she talks about the Lord. If there is one person who is headed for a successful Christian life, Kim is the one.

Summary

The preceding "snapshots" of various Black young adults in different contexts provide us a picture of their lives individually. There are always dangers in such a presentation. Oversimplifying, stereotyping, generalizing, and individualizing are a few.

Keep in mind that any given Black young adult may fit into several categories. Also, Black young adults do not live in isolation from one another. They do have a group life and consequently do need to be observed in the context of interaction with their peers. Finally, what Black young adults **think** is just as important as what they do and how they live. Understanding the thought-life of the Black young adult is crucial for reaching this age group.

Chapter 3

Defining Emergent Black Christian Young Adulthood

Up to this point we have identified and profiled Black young adults. Mostly we have concentrated on Black young adults irrespective of their faith in Christ. It is appropriate for us at this time to define in some detail emergent Black Christian young adulthood. This is our attempt to explicate what we believe could be a "model" Black young adult Christian.

A. Principles Underlying the Definition

In order that careful consideration may be given to our definition and its underlying assumptions, we see fit to take the time to explain two principles which undergird our approach. One factor is Black American identity, and the other is our Christian faith.

1. Black American identity
If it stands to reason that a major difference exists between what it means to be Black in America versus what it means to be white in America, it also stands to reason that a significant

difference exists between being a Black young adult and a white young adult. Historically and sociologically, there has always been a battle in defining Black manhood and womanhood in the American context. Because of racism, Black people in America have always had to fight to rightfully define themselves and to make this definition stick.

Consider the following statement of William H. Bentley in the thesis of his work *The Meaning of History for Black Americans*:

> **"The meaning of history for Blacks in America is to search for and to arrive at a self-definition that takes into account and does full justice to as many of the facts relating to their individual and collective experience in America as are ascertainable, and to achieve the power to make the recognition of that definition define their being"** (National Black Christian Students Conference, 1979, pg. 13).

Care should be taken when defining Black young adulthood within a context of racism. Racism tends to "color" everything, including definitions governing the maturation of persons. For certain, there are basic natural characteristics which govern the growth of all people alike. And the general application of these natural characteristics is better applied to the very young and to the very old of all people. However, the maturative definitions governing those groups falling between the very old and the very young is more relative to values and standards set according to the societies dominant majority than according to natural physiological and emotional characteristics.

For example, a Black male "adolescent" in America may be called a "man" in African culture, but regarded as a "boy" by white America. Further, witness the laws in many states which allow "youth" who commit certain crimes to be tried as "adults" in order that they might receive a greater punishment. And it is common knowledge that, proportionally, more young Black males are in prisons than any other group of Americans.

Another illustration will suffice. In *Understanding People* (E.T.T.A), the authors (following the work of a Robert Havighurst) give eight developmental tasks which they say also serve as "signs of development, or measures of progress" through the young adult stage of experience. These are, 1) selecting a mate (or adjusting to unmarried adult status); 2) learning to live with a marriage partner; 3) starting a family; 4) rearing children (or learning to relate to the children of others); 5) managing a home; 6) getting started in an occupation; 7) taking on civic responsibility; and 8) finding a congenial social group (pg. 76).

Comparing these developmental tasks with the experiences of Black American young adults would leave many of them falling short of the mark of young adulthood, and some entering the phase prematurely. For example, though many Black adolescents are becoming fathers and mothers outside the context of marriage, this does not necessarily confirm them as young *adults*, that is, as possessing the maturity that accompanies the territory. And, "managing a home" would seem to assume a nuclear family consisting of father, mother and children rather than the extended family where several related adults may inhabit the same household. Further, since 60% of Black males between the ages of 18-25 are not employed (and many cannot find employment), the criteria of "getting started in an occupation" would cause many of them to fail to reach young adulthood.

Thus, any meaningful definition of Black young adulthood must take into consideration the bi-cultural context in which Black Americans live and are compelled to relate. This principle underlies our approach. In some respects, the life-experiences of Black young adults differ from those of their white counterparts. And some of these differences are quite marked.

2. The Christian factor
A second principle also underlies our approach. Being straightforward, the definition which we place upon Black young adulthood is influenced by a Christian understanding. Our purpose is to uplift a viable ministry for Black young adults with the purpose in mind of strengthening our

the life of the Christian Black young adult. He needs to know the Lord more intensely than previously in order that Christ may become his sure foundation. This is crucial for the Christian young adult at a time in life when he is pressed to make choices at some major crossroads of life like developing a belief system, constructing a world-life view, selecting a marital partner, and entering into a life's vocation.

The Christian position which we espouse as Black believers leads us to assert that the faith which we love and to which we so dearly cling is capable of fulfilling and guiding the Black young adult. That is, provided the Black young adult reaches his full assurance in this faith.

One reason many of our churches are beset with problems is because many of their members do not have a full assurance of faith. Such lack would be manifested in the lives of members who do not have assurance of their salvation; who do not understand with assurance that heaven awaits them (many a still "trying to make it in"); who do not become active witnesses for Christ because they fear or are unsure of themselves; who cannot pray with confidence because they do not understand the high priestly work of Christ; who do not consistently submit themselves to the Lordship of Jesus Christ, but live by their own unenlightened understanding, etc. Further, many Black young adults fail to come through for Christ and their Church because they have made the wrong decisions at their crossroads and consequently the "cares of this world, and the deceitfulness of riches, and the lusts of other things entering in, choke the word, and it becometh unfruitful" (Mark 4:19).

It is the emergent Black young adult who reaches a full assurance of faith in Christ Jesus who will most benefit our local congregations. The growth will be progressive and ultimately must be wrought by the Holy Spirit. However, when the faith of an emergent young adult reaches its completion, the Church will have gained an invaluable member and servant of the Lord.

5. Maturity in the Black American experience
The progressive growth of the Christian Black young adult, effectuated by God the Holy Spirit, should ultimately "issue

him forth into maturity." A problem with many Black young adults is their lack of maturity. This problem is evidenced in two areas.

One area is general. Basically it concerns the young adult as he or she becomes useful in life. There is a negative element among the Black young adult population who are a "subtraction" from the quality of life in the society in general. These are not about the business of anything substantial. They are idle and vain, making no meaningful contribution to improving the quality of life. By their negative lifestyles they are a hindrance to societal well-being. They take from and use up. They have not matured.

Now this is not meant in any way to even hint at suggesting that these Black young adults who fail to mature should be "written off" by either the society at large or the Black community in particular. Being created in the image and after the likeness of God they possess inherent value as persons of humanity. God loves them and so should we. At the least, these immature Black young adults are a sobering reminder of the failure of the "American Dream" to successfully include and work for all Black Americans. Without excusing their personal responsibility to better themselves, in many ways these Black young adults stand as a witness to the racism and wickedness of this nation.

The other area which manifests the immaturity of Black young adults is more specific. Some Black young adults are not a credit to their race, to the Black American community. These same young adults may be "upwardly mobile," "moving from the ghetto to the 'get-more'," etc. Individualistically, they may have earned themselves a reputation and are becoming well-to-do financially. However, the fruit of their individual success is enjoyed by them alone. More or less, the Black group as a whole does not benefit from the progress of it's individual achievers.

This is why the maturation process of emergent Black Christian young adulthood is to be measured "in the context of the Black American experience." **If Black Christian young adults are not developed in such a way that their lives will be useful for strengthening the quality of life for Black people in America, then Black Christian education has**

40

failed in this area. It takes far more substance to mature a young adult whose life is beneficial to the Black community than it does to mature a young adult whose life is beneficial to himself alone. And furthermore, we are not certain that we can rightfully call the latter "maturity."

(a) Overcoming the vanities of adolescence void of Christ

> *"I write unto you, young men, because*
> *ye have overcome the wicked one"*
> *(1 John 2:13b, 14c).*

This maturity of emergent Christian Black young adulthood should be demonstrated and reflected in three areas. First, it is shown in the young adult "overcoming the vanities of adolescence void of Christ." The Scripture teaches us that "childhood and youth are vanity" (Ecclesiastes 11:10). To become a genuine young adult one must forsake the vanities associated with adolescence. As the Apostle Paul stated, "When I was a child, I talked like a child, I thought like a child, I reasoned like a child. When I became a man, I put childish ways behind me" (1 Corinthians 13:11, NIV).

Adolescence in itself is not inherently corruptible. Adolescence is the common term identifying the phase of life entered when a person leaves youthhood (around 12 or 13) and before they enter young adulthood. It has physical content (puberty), but it also has Black American cultural and social content. Adolescence can and should be a natural phase of growth for young people.

It is the "adolescence void of Christ" that is harmful to the development of wholesome young people. And if not corrected the excess baggage of this adolescence will be carried right into young adulthood. It is constantly happening all around us in the Black community. We see numerous young men and women who persist in acting as teenagers, who in many ways refuse to "grow up."

Secular Black adolescence is destroying generation after generation of precious Black young adults. By the time some

Black adolescents reach young adulthood, their lives have already been wasted — body, mind, and spirit. **Consequently, at the time these young adults should be joining forces with the Black adult population to further develop and strengthen their people, they themselves have become candidates for redemption.**

Black adolescents who do not genuinely have Christ are wiped out through drugs, alcoholism, miseducation, historical ignorance, psychological emasculation, low-self esteem, sexual irresponsibility, a no-work ethic, individualistic and immoral values, and the like. This is shown through gang-life, running the street, idleness relative to purpose and work, unwed fathers and mothers, high school drop-outs, worshiping basketball, following effeminate idols and consciously unBlack music stars, etc.

With Christ Jesus and His values, the Black adolescent can mature through the period of adolescence. When he reaches young adulthood he can be ready, through the help of Christ, to make the most of the experience, fully anticipating assuming the full role of a Black adult.

"I write unto you, young men, because
ye have overcome *the wicked one"*
(1 John 2:13b, 14c).

(b) Exercising and exhibiting strength in living

"I have written unto you, young men, because
ye are strong..."
(1 John 2:14b).

Second, the maturity of emergent Black Christian young adulthood should be demonstrated and reflected in the young adult "exercising and exhibiting strength in living." It is sad to see young men and women who are beat down by life. Physically, many young adults are already ruined. One senior citizen who had been hospitalized offered to surrender her bed to a young adult. Her comment afterwards, "The older people were healthier than the young people."

Psychologically, emotionally and socially we see the same. Black young adults do not have a "Black" cause into which they have channeled their energies and to which they have abandoned themselves. The power manifested by many Black young adults involved in the civil rights movement of the 60's clearly overshadows what is being manifested today. During the present time, the social resistance and militancy of the 60's generation is gone, especially in the lives of Black males. An article in Essence magazine (November '85; William Strickland) raised the question, "Where have all the Black warriors Gone?" The article stated that the historical battle of Blacks in this country rages on, but many of the warriors are gone. According to the needs of their times, former generations of Blacks sought "freedom" in terms of returning to Africa; struggling against slavery; fighting against the caste system in the South and prejudice and discrimination in the North; fighting for full civil and human rights; fighting for the unhindered right to vote; and working for Black power. But contemporarily, most Black young adults do not have the strength to fight, and they have yet to defined what "freedom" for Blacks means for their generation.

Some Black young men and women do not even have the strength to live. Witness the rising number of physical suicides occurring among Black young people and young adults. This is not to mention the slow form of suicide taking place through the widespread use of drugs by members in the Black community.

Where can a young adult receive the will and power to live, and to be a warrior and overcomer in life? We answer, from Christ. Emergent Black young adults need the spiritual power given by the Lord Christ Jesus. The Scripture teaches, "Be on your guard; stand firm in the faith; be men of courage; be strong" (1 Corinthians 16:13, NIV). The maturity manifested in the life of spiritual "young men" can be gained by the Black young adult.

"*I have written unto you, young men, because*
ye are strong..." *(1 John 2:14b).*

(c) Internalizing and appropriating the values of God as expressed in His Word

"I have written unto you, young men, because...
the word of God abideth in you"
(1 John 2:14c).

Third, the maturity of emergent Black Christian young adulthood should be demonstrated and reflected in the young adult "internalizing and appropriating the values of God as expressed in His word." This is an indispensable part of our definition.

As mentioned previously, those who are young adults have affectively determined their values and are following a course of life that is accordant with those values. Young adults are not as "set in their ways" as older adults. However, they are getting there in a hurry.

Matter of fact, young children, youth, young people and young adults are increasingly developing faster at earlier ages. For example, because of extreme socio-economic pressures, many Black children are not enjoying the joys of childhood as former generations did. And through the mass media, some early and middle adolescents have already been exposed to aspects of life which previously were reserved for adults. Some act as "grown" as adults, and in some cases (at initial meetings) one is hardly able to tell the difference.

The emergent Christian young adult's values must be shaped, and in some cases replaced by biblical Christian values. Many of today's Christian young adults unconsciously profess and practice non-Christian values. For example, one reason some single Christian young adults engage in the act of fornication (an act the Scripture clearly prohibits) is because they have not been taught God's truth as it relates to sexuality. The same could be said for "cheating" on educational exams, which many commonly regard as an acceptable matter of course toward achieving the goal of graduation. Value-wise, little consideration is given to the fact that such behavior is regressive from the standards of ethical, moral and academic excellence.

Emergent Christian Black young adults need to "hear" the Word of God. They need to audibly hear it, they need to spiritually hear it in their understanding, and they need to hear it speaking through their lives and in their experiences. That is,

44

the values taught by precept and example in the written Word need to be internalized and appropriated in their lives. This should be done through the power of the Holy Spirit who is "the Spirit of truth," and should occur both on the individual and the group levels.

"I have written unto you, young men, because...
the word of God abideth in you"
(1 John 2:14c)

6. Christ-centered Black adulthood

Those who teach and minister to Black Christian young adults should desire to bring them into "a mature Black adulthood of which Christ is the center." For at some time or another, the young adult will eventually become and be regarded as a full-fledged adult, with no "young" attached. (This phase of maturation should be attained by the young adult somewhere between ages 25-34, age 35 being a commencing point of middle-adulthood.)

When this step of maturation is reached, the Lord Christ Jesus, both in the person of His Spirit and in the principles of His Word, should dwell and rule preeminently in the life of the adult man or woman. This aspect of Christ-centered adult maturation should be unswervingly held to by the adult and unmistakably recognized by others.

Of the several characteristics identifying adults, we choose to highlight two. The adult who has emerged from Christian Black young adulthood should possess a "settled and servanthood" posture.

(a) A Settled posture

The Christ-centered Black adult should be settled. He should be stable and established. Whatever was needed in order to fulfill one's purpose and life-calling should have been acquired. The "will of God" in terms of its practical manifestation for the adult man or woman should have been identified, and a path for fulfilling this will should have been implemented. This is not to suggest that when the emergent young adult reaches adulthood he should then have accomplished most of what he is going to accomplish in life. It is only to say that the foundation for his life as an adult should have been established and established well.

Christ-centered adulthood, if it has matured, is a time to work and to build. Preparation was before, realization is now. Whatever lasting marks in the sands of time the Black Christian adult is going to make in life, he should be prepared to make during the years immediately following young adulthood. For it seems that in this phase of life he will either lapse into actual mediocrity or abound in productivity.

(b) A Servanthood posture

The Christ-centered Black adult should also be a servant. If the life of the Black Christian young adult has been adequately prepared, then the life of the Christ-centered Black adult will manifest itself in service, especially to the Black community.

A mature adult is a servant. A genuine Christian is a servant. Witness the servanthood posture of Jesus as described in the *Kenosis* ("emptying") passage, Philippians 2:1-16 (especially vv. 5-11). Servanthood was a virtue which Jesus constrained His close followers to assume (cf. Matthew 20:20-28; 23:11-12; Mark 9:33-37; 10:35-45; Luke 22:24-27; John 13:1-16).

If there is one thing that the Black community in America needs, it is Black Christian adults who are dedicated servants of their people first, and all others second. Jesus said, "Thou shalt love thy neighbor as thyself" (Matthew 22:39b). The Scripture teaches that if a Christian person is capable but does not care for his own relatives and family he has denied the faith (1 Timothy 5:8). The prophet Isaiah proclaimed that one aspect of the Lord's chosen fast is "that thou hide not thyself from thine own flesh" (58:7c).

This quality of Christian Black adults who become servants of their people is the kind who will most benefit Black America and the world.

Summary

The foregoing is our explanation of the definition of "emergent Black Christian young adulthood." Perhaps there are some who for a variety of reasons would take exception with all or part of this objective. We would trust at any rate, that this definition would be given careful consideration. We think it is both comprehensive and gets to the heart of the issues facing young Black Americans. In the interests of openness and honesty we have attempted to clear the ground.

At the least this definition can be used as a starting point from which to formulate an objective and some meaningful aims, as well as a viable program to reach and further teach Black young adults.

Having clearly stated the basis for our treatment of this subject, we can now turn our attention toward providing some additional insights into how best we can reach and teach the group we know as Black young adults. Particularly, the definition of emergent Black Christian young adulthood will be turned into an objective and several aims. Also, we will provide more information geared toward helping the emerging young adult to properly emerge. As various ideas are suggested the reader should remember that this part of the writing is the foundation into which our other ideas are rooted.

REACHING AND TEACHING BLACK YOUNG ADULTS

Second Part

Reaching Black Young Adults

Introduction

In the first part of this book we covered understanding Black young adults and were provided with a definition encapsulating emergent Black Christian young Adulthood. This definition, in essence, becomes an objective guiding the ministry of Black Christian educators of Black young adults.

However, before we can teach Black young adults, we must first reach them. The question we are constantly asking ourselves is how best can this be done?

Chapter 4

Reaching Those in the Church

A. Start with the young adults already within your grasp.

This is an important key to reaching young adults. This demonstrates the principle of faithfulness. If we are faithful in developing the little we possess, the Lord will bless us with more to develop. If your Church has only two or three young adults, begin relating to them.

Do not neglect your junior and senior high school students. If the Church effectively holds them, they will become the nucleus of the young adult group in a couple of years. Look upon these young people as your potential young adults. And begin to think early of the type of programs they will need in order to stay close to the Church.

B. Develop and nurture the consciousness among the young adults that they are a distinct group in the Church.

Young adults are no longer young people, i.e. older adolescents. Neither are they older adults. They are who they are, young adults. Nurture their in-group cohesion. Usually young adults are integrated into the work of the Church person by person. However, there may be a better way.

1. Using the group structure

The Church at which the author is a member (First Baptist Congregational Church, Chicago, IL) is composed of twelve groups. Each new Church member is assigned to a particular group. This apportioning is especially important with the young children, youth, and young people. It is crucial with the young adults.

The young adults (those past the high school age), are placed in a group with their peers. (Though some churches do the same through their young adult choir, the group structure seems better. Every young adult does not sing in the choir.) Thus, the young adults immediately have role models with which to identify.

Now we know that placing young adults in a group by themselves may be threatening and intimidating to some of the older Church members. Young adults do have a lot of energy and ideas, and have great potential. The potential for divisiveness in such an order is most apparent. However, if this group is handled correctly, and has the right kind of leadership, this kind of order can become a rich blessing for the Church.

Unlike the other adult groups of the Church, the population of the young adult group will change. For the young adult eventually will become a full adult. And it is at this point of maturity that individual young adults are moved from the young adult group and placed into positions of service in the other adult groups.

2. The benefit of the group structure

The genius of the young adult group lies in the fact that it is a holding and developing body. Its membership is not meant to remain static. At different stages this group may be the largest group in the Church. But that is one of the benefits it serves. For the more young adults a Church has, the more young adults a Church will receive. Young adults will attract other young adults.

Periodically, over the months and years, young adults will

50

be phased out of the young adult group and phased into other adult groups, as well as into leadership positions in the Church. There will be no need to rush the removal of young adults from their group to another. Allow time for them to develop as strong Christian men and women. Then place them when they are ready.

3. The leadership of the young adult group

The person responsible for leading the young adults in any given Church should be carefully chosen. Black young adults will not just sit around patiently enduring the kind of leadership which speaks down to them, "preaches" to them all the time, does not know what is happening in their world, etc. Rather than waste their time and continually be insulted, the young adults will go somewhere else. It takes a mature Christian person to lead young adults.

Also, the leader of young adults should understand the nature of the Church which is the Body of Christ. His purpose is not to instigate division in the Church through the influence he exerts over this age group. He should promote unity in the Church. He should not follow the example of Absalom, who, as a good looking young man stole the hearts of the men of Israel from King David his father (cf. 2 Samuel 15:1-6).

C. Stay in close touch with any students who go away to college.

Many Black congregations lose their young adults when their high school graduates enter college away from home. Yet, this situation need not persist. We believe it can be checked if a Church is willing to stay in touch with its college students who attend schools in other areas.

It should not be hard to locate someone in your congregation (preferably one who has been working with the senior high age group) who is willing to invest the kind of time necessary to stay in touch with college students away from home. One might think that concern shown by the student's parents would suffice. However, not every student who attends college has a parent who is an active Church member. Furthermore, a student takes it for granted that his parent will show concern for him while he is away from home. This is why contact made with a student by a non-relative can leave a great impression.

We have all heard the saying, "Everybody's responsibility is nobody's responsibility." Thus, it is necessary to place this area of service into the hands of a faithful member who will do the work it requires. (College students can so easily be forgotten.) This person can write, call, mail "care packages," send cassette tapes of Church services, and do other things which both keep the student informed about what is happening at the Church and let him know that the Church values his membership and is concerned for his success as a college student.

Some churches have the kind of financial resources available that might allow the person coordinating a ministry to college students to visit with those students who are away from home. Consider the exciting possibilities of someone from your church making the circuit of the colleges where your students are located. Such a person could spend a day with this student, or two days with that student providing fellowship and counseling. Just think of the impact such a well-planned personal visit would have on a student.

The aim is to stay in close contact with your students who are away from home. If your church continues to reach these students while they are away, then, all things being equal, you can expect these students to return to their Church during summer vacations and when they graduate. If substantial help (material and otherwise) has been provided these students, then the Church can expect that they will show their appreciation in ways they are able. Also, the Church can then with integrity call on its students to reinvest themselves in their Church and community, for the Church will have assisted them through their educational development.

Chapter 5

Reaching the Unchurched - I
Win the Unsaved to Christ and
then to the Church

Introduction

There are three kinds of unchurched young adults whom the Church can reach. The first is the unsaved, the second is the backslider, and the third is the away-from-home college student. This chapter covers the former group and the following chapter will cover the latter two groups.

Young adults who are not saved must be brought to salvation first and then into Church membership. Evangelism is the means of bringing all the lost to Christ, including young adults. Evangelism is simply bringing to the lost the message and ministry of the Good News of Jesus Christ in such a way that they repent from their sins, turn to Him in saving faith, and accept Him as Lord and Liberator of their lives.

A. Actively Evangelize Young Adults

One sure way to reach young adults is to go out and win them to Christ. The day has passed when many young adults seek out the Church. Many churches will be waiting forever, if they expect numerous Black young adults to invade the Church. There are just too many other things which have captured the interest of Black young adults. The Church must actively engage herself in evangelizing this age group, especially since those in this group can generally be found "where the action is."

In order to reach young adults with the Gospel, serious attention should be given to showing the relevance of the Gospel to their experience. As Christ Jesus said to the Church in the city of Pergamum, "I know where you live," (Revelation 2:13, NIV), so must the Black Church be prepared to say the same to the young adults of Black America. We should know, and know well, where they live. And if we do, and they know that we do, they will be more ready to hear the message of salvation that we bring.

B. Make Black Males a Special Emphasis

1. They are missing from the Church

Of particular interest in the evangelization of Black young adults is the concern for reaching the Black male. It is common knowledge that the Black male is proportionately more absent from the Black Church than the Black female. It is high time for the Black Church to ask "Why?" this is so. Let us suggest several reasons.

Somewhere along the line, perhaps especially during the decade of the 60's, the Church became irrelevant to and out of touch with the Black male. Perhaps the Church was perceived more as a problem than an help to the struggles of Black people in America, in which struggles many young Black males were actively engaged. The Black Church has not recovered from the charge forcefully propagated in the '60's by many Blacks that the Bible is the "white man's book," and that Christianity is the "white man's religion" useful for keeping Black people in place. Consequently, successive generations of Black males have continued to emulate those who had nothing to do with the Church. This has resulted in the manifestation of several generations of Black males having no Church background whatsoever.

2. Change the image of the Church and its leadership

The image of Christianity practiced by Blacks in America needs to be redefined to Black men. Socially, the Church in the community needs to be perceived as being aligned with the ministry of God in the world that brings freedom for those who are oppressed and help for those who are struggling. As Black men see the Church projecting this renewed image, we believe they will be attracted to Christ. This has been the resultant fruit when progressive pastors lead their churches into works of social action and community ministry: they eventually attract Black men. And not just any Black men. These men are strong.

Perhaps more crucial than the image projected by the Church is the image projected by the leader of the Church, the minister. Whether we choose to accept it or not, there are many Black males who do not choose to identify with the Church because they are offended by the immoral conduct of the preacher. Though this is not the only reason why many Black males "boycott" the Church, it is important enough for us to consider. The matter is quite serious.

For instance, when word gets out on the street that some ministers have been legally charged with dealing drugs from the pulpit (even though only a few of all ministers have been involved in the illegal traffic), how does this affect the perception of the integrity of the ministry? It is worth mentioning that when the author desired to know what was going down in any Church in the community, all that was necessary for him to do was ask the fellows on the street. To a certain degree they had the inside word on all the negative actions and activities of the ministers.

The fact remains that there is a correlation between how the preacher lives and the Church attendance of Black males. So if the Church endeavors to reach the male Black young adult, the Church must call its minister to strive to live a life "void of offense" (cf. Acts 24:16; 2 Corinthians 6:3; 1 Corinthians 10:32).

3. Pray and brainstorm

Now it is quite certain that neither all Black congregations nor those who lead them are modeling negative images to all

Black males. There are many churches which have a reasonably strong Black male membership and a strong manhood emphasis. However, there are other good churches which, despite their goodness, still fail to attract any sizable number of Black young adult men.

It would seem that our churches need to make this a subject of much prayer and brainstorming. It is most spiritually disturbing when the churches of any ethnic group do not command the attention, respect and commitment of the men belonging to that group. What is it about Black churches that does not attract Black men? How can this situation be remedied before those Black men who are at least neutral to our churches turn to become antagonistic toward them? Further, how shall the leadership of our churches continue to face single young adult Black Christian women when we lack the influence to win and Christianly educate for them Black men who become good men, husbands and fathers?

C. Biblical Models for Reaching Men on the Street

Countless Black males can be found lingering in the streets of cities where Blacks reside. The way of the street is their life, and if they are to be won to Christ and to His Church, they must be approached in the street where they are found. There are several biblical models useful for inspiring those who would evangelize persons whose lives are centered in the street.

1. Jephthah, the son of a prostitute

One model for reaching Black males in the street is that of Jephthah (Judges 10:6-12:7). Jephthah was a mighty warrior, the son of a prostitute. He was ostracized by his half-brothers who were the offspring of Jephthah's father Gilead and his wife.

Jephthah was a person who knew God and the history of his people. He also exhibited good leadership abilities. Some of the "worthless fellows" (11:4) joined themselves with Jephthah and went raiding with him. His life could be characterized as a "street life."

There came a time when the people of God needed the services of Jephthah. They needed his help to defeat the Ammonites who were making war against them. At first Jephthah scolded them for their mistreatment of himself. Up until this point they had hated him and forced him to leave his community. But now that they were in trouble they had come to him for help. Yet, Jephthah, despite how he had been treated, decided to help his people, provided that if he were successful they would make him their leader.

The rest is history. Jephthah defeated the Ammonites in battle and subsequently became a judge of the people for six years. Jephthah's name has come down to the Christian community as a person of great faith (cf. Hebrews 11:32). The lesson for us is that God can redeem those in the street and use them in His service as successful community activists.

2. David, a fugitive

Another model which can encourage those who seek to win to Christ those persons living the street life is that of David. David was the second king of Israel. However, before David became king he spent many years being chased around the countryside by a jealous and demoniacal king Saul, who knew that God had numbered his days.

When David escaped from Achish the king of Gath by feigning madness, he departed into the cave of Adullam. When his brothers and kinfolks got news where David was, they came to him. Some other persons also came and joined themselves with David. The Scripture says "every one who was in distress, and every one who was in debt, and every one who was discontented, gathered to him; and he became captain over them. And there were with him about four hundred men" (1 Samuel 22:2, RSV; cf. 21:12-22:2). In another place the Scripture calls these men "wicked and base fellows" (1 Samuel 30:22, RSV). This group sounds as though they could have come straight from the streets of Chicago, New York, Philadelphia, or the like.

We can trace the movements of David and these men through several passages. 1 Samuel 23:13 says that David and his men, who had grown to a group of 600, went wherever they could go when they left Keilah. From 1 Samuel 13:29 and 24:22

we learn that they encamped at the stronghold of Engedi. And in 1 Samuel 25:13 we learn that 400 of David's men went up to fight against Nabal while 200 stayed behind with their baggage. From the passage which has this latter verse we receive an interesting picture of David's men. By this time they were so well disciplined that they committed no wreckless violence nor stole from others, even when they had the obvious advantage (cf. 25:5-7, 14-16, 21).

The next Scripture mentioning David's men is 1 Chronicles 12:1 ff. This passage clearly identifies "the men who came to David at Ziklag, while he could not move freely because of Saul the son of Kish" with being "among the mighty men who helped him in war" (RSV). Verses 2 and following proceed to personally identify these men and extol their abilities (cf. vv. 3, 8, 16, 19, 20-22). (The parallel passage, 1 Samuel 27:2-6 sheds additional insights about David and his men.)

The lesson is clear. David's "street men" — the distressed, the indebted, and the discontented — ultimately became transformed into his "mighty men." And these were the mighty men who led the army of David in bringing victory to the people of God. Through their association with David these men became a force for the liberation of their people.

God is able to save, transform and use in service Black young adults whose pattern of living is centered in the street culture. However, it takes men of courage and faith to win them and work with them. Yet, it can be done.

D. Reach into the Prisons

We can also reach male (and female) Black young adults through ministry in the prison. For this is where many of them can be located, in numbers far out of proportion to the general population of Black Americans.

1. Black males will listen

Not all Black males in prison are there because they have violated the law. Some were railroaded. Not all Black males are, nor desire to be, repeat offenders. Some, by virtue of the shock of their prison experience, never want to be locked up again. Some, when they get out, want to stay out. And the Church hopes that they will indeed stay out.

But while these young adult Black males are in prison they will listen to those who know the truth. As the Psalmist said, "Some were living in gloom and darkness, prisoners suffering in chains, because they had rebelled against the commands of Almighty God and had rejected his instructions. They were worn out from hard work; they would fall down, and no one would help. Then in their trouble they called to the Lord, and he saved them from their distress. He brought them out of their gloom and darkness and broke their chains in pieces" (107:10-14, TEV).

2. Invest some regular time

One of our fellow ministers (Rev. Clarence Hilliard, pastor of Austin Corinthian Baptist Church, Chicago, IL) spends more than half a day each week at the Cook County House of Corrections, (Chicago, IL). There he conducts services and counsels with the young adult men. Many have given their lives to the Lord, and they look forward to his coming each week.

Sooner or later most Black inmates will be released. And the odds would indicate that if they should seek a Church home, they will find their way to the Church who came to minister to them. Now a prison ministry may not evidence immediate results for a local congregation. But the ministry is well worth it. And in the long run a Church may gain several key Black males who will become instrumental in bringing others similar to themselves into the Church. Nevertheless, remember the words of Jesus: *"I was in prison and you came to visit me"* (Matthew 25:36c, NIV).

3. Minister to those released

Also, all over America the Chaplains in the prisons where many Black males are located are looking for churches which will be willing to follow-up on those who win parole. They are really grasping for the services of congregations who care. Church members who feel called to such a ministry could write letters, make phone calls, make personal visits, and give invitations for these former inmates to come to church.

It is important too for the Church to be sensitive to those who have been incarcerated. For they must be nurtured carefully and not despised or treated with contempt because of their prison experience. The Church doors and the hearts of Church members should be open to receive these former inmates into the fellowship. This is the only way their lives will be fully redeemed.

Chapter 6

Reaching the Unchurched - II
Win the Backslider and the College Student

A. Win the Backslider to Restoration and then to the Church

The second kind of young adults whom the Church is able to reach are the backsliders. They must first be brought to restoration with the Lord and then restoration into the Church.

Not every Black young adult who is absent from the Church is without knowledge of salvation through Jesus Christ. Some know the Lord and know they are wrong in being away from the Lord and His people. Nevertheless, they find themselves on the outside of the local congregation. And they need to come back home.

1. Be sensitive and prayerful
It takes a mature Christian to win the backslider back into fellowship with the Lord. The one who would win the backslider must be prayerful and sensitive to his experience. Somewhere in the backslider's past he ran into a stumbling block or took a wrong turn that helped to draw him away from Christ. In many cases the proper kind of foundation was not laid in his life for living a faithfully successful life as a believer in Christ. That is, he was not taught the importance of daily prayer and Bible study, dependence on the Holy Spirit, partaking the

Lord's Supper, or being faithful to the Church fellowship.

2. Understand their weaknesses

Many backsliders, those who really know the Lord as their Savior, know that they arc out of their rightful place and, deep within, do not really want to be where they are. Their heart probably condemns them more than they would like to admit. We must be sensitive to them and help them. What went wrong in their lives? Maybe it was the death of a close relative. It could have been a broken love relationship. Perhaps someone they respected a lot let them down hard. Probably it was some kind of habitual sin which they did not know the Holy Spirit would eventually cleanse from their life.

The key is to be sensitive and show love. Think about the young man, Lot, who became a backslider. Consider his experience. For if God "rescued Lot, a righteous man, who was distressed by the filthy lives of lawless men (for that righteous man, living among them day after day, was tormented in his righteous soul by the lawless deed he saw and heard) — if this is so, then the Lord knows how to rescue godly men from trials" (2 Peter 2:7-8, NIV).

The prodigal son is another example of a young adult who turned away from the Lord. It does not take much insight to see that once this young adult man had fallen to his lowest, he was desperate to get back home. If his father had not been sensitive and loving he would have pitifully crushed any hope which lingered in his son. Yet, his father was forgiving and kind, and welcomed fully his son back home (cf. Luke 15:11-24).

3. Make regular visitations

Has it ever occurred to you that many unchurched persons are actively staying away from some particular Church? And the Church which you attend may be just the one that some Black young adult is staying away from. What this means is that when the Lord finally does get the message through to His wayward child that it is the time for him to get squared away with the Lord, he has already decided that so-and-so Church is the place he will return.

This means that it is important for a Church to do regular visitations through the community where it is located, to achieve optimum exposure to the backslider. (Some cults in our community get their exposure every week.) It is known that one key to successful advertising is to keep one's product in the eye of the public so that when the need or desire for the product finally arises, this product will be revealed just at the opportune time. Then the consumer will make a conscious choice to get that product. The last word heard is often the first word acted upon. Therefore, visit, Church, visit. And reach the young adult backslider when the time for him is right.

B. Persuade the College Student from out of town to submit to Watchcare

1. They need an older support group

Throughout the country, especially in some large metropolitan areas, there are many Black students who are away from their homes. Some of these students attended the services of a Church where they came from. All of them need some kind of significant support group other than their peers. Local congregations can do a great service by providing a watchcare ministry for Black college students away from home.

Especially within a big city, there is nothing to compare with a college student living on campus having a group of few "home-like folks" who can welcome him into a warm fellowship. Those of us who at some point of our lives have been secluded on a campus away from home can testify to the value of having somewhere else to go and someone else to turn to for.

2. Make significant contact

What kinds of practical things can the Church do for the Black college student away from his home? The Church can embark on a "search and secure" mission. Get into contact with the colleges/universities in your area. The fall enrollment time (late August, early September) is opportune.

Send a male-female team from your Church to where the

students gather. Have some kind of literature identifying your Church and its services. Include numbers to call in an emergency. Also, have some kind of a "care package" of little things which students can use. And don't forget something like some homemade deserts (cookies, sweet potato pie, etc.). Give these items as gifts of care and concern to the students you meet.

3. Be of assistance
If you are able to secure the student's phone number and location, follow up. See if he has run into any special problems or have any special needs. Be of assistance if you can. Perhaps those who made the initial contact can offer to show the student or group of students around the city. This can be a real winner if it is done before the students get into the business of hectic study.

4. Invite them to church
Invite the students to your Church and offer to pick them up if necessary. Following the service, arrange for some family to have the students over for dinner. If dinner is served at Church the pastor and his wife (or the pastor and her husband!) can host the out-of-town guests at his table. Without being pushy, try to determine the spiritual state of the student(s). Do they need to know the Lord? Were they regular in attendance at the services of the Church in the city where they reside? Do they realize the kind of watchcare they need or are they prone to drift? Were they involved in service in their Church back home, and is there anything they can do to strengthen your Church?

5. Follow through
Once initial contact has been made, the male-female team can keep the ball rolling. Remember, food, money (college students always have needs), and spiritual counsel are good drawing cards for a Church in search of Black young adult college students. Be creative, and don't fail to offer special prayers for these students. Whether they know the Lord or not, most will appreciate your Church's concern.

6. Reap long-range rewards

If a Church is successful in reaching out to college students who are away from home, and are able to win some to Christ and or into the fellowship of the Church, the results will be most rewarding. If a student is planning to attend college for four years, then the Church may have gained itself a faithful member and worker. Plus, college students influence other college students. So in three or four years your "Saturday night college young adult fellowship," for example, may grow from two or three to more than twenty students. Finally, oftentimes students who go away to college find employment and stay in the area of their educational institution following their graduation. If your Church has won such a student to Christ and/or membership in your Church, it is possible that your Church may have gained a good member for many years to come.

Chapter 7

Reaching the Unchurched - III
Develop young adult interest centers for the unemployed especially

A. The Idle Unemployed

There are many unemployed Black young adults. Many of these unemployed Black males stay idle in the street. And many of the Black females remain at home glued to their "stories." This is too much time and energy going to waste. Churches could develop interest centers that would attract these unemployed young adults.

B. The Purposes served by Interest Centers

Such interest centers could serve several purposes. One would be to actively involve young adults in programs that would better equip them to enter the job market. Another could be to serve as a center of informal education and information sharing. Interest centers could also serve the purpose of inspiring and challenging the young adults to exercise their creativity in production.

The underlying aim of this kind of program would be to both evangelize the lost as well as preserve and develop the basic humanity and potential of Black young adults.

C. What the Church should be Ready To Do

The opening of an interest center does require a commitment from the Church. It almost assumes the full-time status of a pastor and at least a volunteer staff of Church members who will dedicate their time to developing specific aspects of a program and to teaching and facilitating. Also, the Church must have the right kind of space in order to house the program, and be willing to set aside seed money to operate the program. This will be especially taxing during the winter months of the heating season.

D. Ideas for Programs

Following are some of the kinds of things which could be accomplished through an interest center. Much could be done in order to equip the unemployed young adult to secure meaningful employment. Such a program could include brush-up tutoring in reading and math, filling out job applications, preparing resumes, preparing for job interviews, sharing leads and other information, etc.

Educational groups could be structured for unwed mothers, for example. Such groups could discuss common concerns and problems in the area of child discipline, male role models for their children, managing a budget, child development, etc.

Creative production groups could also be formulated. With the proper kind of guidance, much of the creativity of the unemployed could be geared toward developing ways and means to make a living outside the area of available employment. For instance, most women wear some kind of jewelry. Provided with the basic materials and working tools, there is no good reason an interest group could not begin some type of production and marketing of inexpensive jewelry. Other kinds of light production could also be engaged in for profit to be shared by those in the interest center.

E. Any Results will be Worth It

What is important in this respect is remembering that it is

through the interest centers that the Church is trying to reach the idle young adult. Whatever advances made along these lines will be welcomed. As it presently stands, many Black young adults are not inspired to involve themselves in anything else beside the street and the "stories." Thus any basic but good program the Church starts will serve to draw these young adults from that pattern of life which does little to contribute to their further growth.

Perhaps from the outset only a few young adults will be gained to the Church through such programs. Nevertheless, having these few is better than not having them. And if we seriously think through the implications of the thousands of unemployed in our community, we would realize that their idleness is financially costing the Church week after week. For in many ways, it is Black congregations which are absorbing the burden of caring for many of these unemployed young adults through the supportive services of food, clothing, love offerings, interceding for those who get caught up in crime, etc.

REACHING AND TEACHING BLACK YOUNG ADULTS

Third Part

Teaching Black Young Adults

Introduction

Understanding Black young adults enables us to *reach* them. And reaching Black young adults (if we are able to keep them) provides us with the possibility of being able *teach* them. The kinds of questions that are raised for us at this juncture are: What should be our objective when teaching Black young adults? What kinds of things should young adults be taught? What are the best ways to effectively teach Black young adults?, etc. In this final part we will try to provide some answers for questions like these.

The reader should understand that when we speak of "teaching" Black young adults we are discussing more than disseminating information to the learner. Basically, of course, we most certainly are talking about disseminating the truth of God's Word to young adults. However, our understanding of teaching may also involve developing young adults in terms of their potential, energizing them into obedient faith and action, empowering them to do service and exercise leadership in the Church, preparing them for the future, and equipping them for the work of the ministry (cf. Ephesians 4:12f.)

Let us be reminded that young adults are in an emerging phase of growth. The entrance of the young person into young adulthood is comparable to a "resurrection" in gradual process. Their continuance as a young adult is comparable to a "40" day confirmation period. And their entrance into adulthood is comparable to an "ascension." The content of the teaching which young adults receive will be the determining factor as to whether they are genuinely affirmed as young adults and ascend properly into adulthood.

Chapter 8

Starting with an Objective and Aims

A. An Objective for Teaching Christian Black Young Adults

As we begin this third and final section we should first take the definition of emergent Black Christian young adulthood and form it into an objective for young adults. This objective will guide the Church's teaching ministry to this age group.

Consider the following as an objective of a church's ministry to its Black young adults.

A Church's Objective

To oversee the spiritual growth of its young adults through that developmental stage of life known as young adulthood in such a way that each of them will receive the full assurance of faith in Jesus Christ, leave fully the period of adolescence, achieve wholistic maturity as a young adult Black American, and become prepared to live the life of a Christ-centered middle adult.

B. Five Aims to Accomplish in the lives of Christian Black Young Adults

This objective for the Christian education of Black young adults can be delineated into several aims.

1. The aims stated

Aim 1: Break with adolescence,
appreciate young adulthood
To aid each Black male and each Black female in making a healthful and clean break with their thinking and pattern of life as an adolescent so that they can be accepted and come to appreciate the status of being a genuine Christian Black young adult.

Aim 2: Grow into full assurance,
reevaluate your faith
To provide prayerful, consultative, and careful support for each Christian Black young adult as he endeavors to grow into the full assurance of faith in Jesus Christ while proceeding through the transition of reevaluating his faith, particularly as it relates to his reassessing, resecuring, and reasserting his convictions in the areas of confirming his salvation, renewing his commitment to Christ, reaffirming his belief system, and constructing his world-life view.

Aim 3: Mature wholistically,
be assured in God's will
To assist Christian Black young adults in becoming wholistically mature by learning as believers in Christ how to become fully assured in all the will of God particularly as it relates to both their dealing

with the crucial choices/courses of action facing them, their questions, problems, and experiences of life besetting them as Black Americans (understood in both their historical and contemporary contexts), and their learning and starting to fulfill the important part they stand to play in strengthening and helping their Church and their people.

Aim 4: Depend on the Holy Spirit, appropriate the Word
To help each Christian Black young adult to understand and practice the importance and value of depending on the Holy Spirit and internalizing and appropriating the values of the Word of God in order to progressively and properly mature as a Christian Black young adult.

Aim 5: Settle into adulthood, serve Christ and people
To inspire and urge Christian Black young adults to as soon as possible become settled as middle adults so that they and/or their families can become fully involved in the work of Christ in their Church and the world, especially as His work involves their service to their own Black people.

2. The aims highlighted

(a) Concerning Aim 1:
Break with adolescence, appreciate young adulthood
The following Scripture indicates in no uncertain terms that an adult person should make a break with the period of youthhood.

1 Corinthians 13:11   "When I was a child, I talked like a child, I thought like a child, I reasoned like a child. When I became a man, I put childish ways behind me." (NIV)

Ecclesiastes 11:9-10   "Rejoice, O young man, in your youth, and let your heart cheer you in the days of your youth; walk in the ways of your heart and the sight of your eyes. But know that for all these things God will bring you into judgment. Remove vexation from your mind, and put away pain from your body; for youth and the dawn of life are vanity." (RSV)

2 Timothy 2:22   "Flee the evil desires of youth, and pursue righteousness, faith, love and peace, along with those who call on the Lord out of a pure heart." (NIV)

Judges 8:18-21   Though this is a passage about the cruel realities of war, it provides an example of a man who thought his oldest son had grown into manhood. The man's name was Gideon, and his oldest son was named Jether. Two Midianite kings, Zebah and Zalmunna, were captured by Gideon after they had killed Gideon's brothers during the fighting. Revenging the death of his brothers, Gideon told his son Jether to "'Rise, and slay them.' But the youth did not draw his sword; for he was afraid, because he was still a youth. Then Zebah and Zalmunna said, 'Rise yourself, and fall upon us; for as the man is, so is his strength." (RSV)

(b) Concerning Aim 2:
Grow into full assurance, reevaluate your faith

The following texts provide a basis for a Christian's reexamination of his own life with Christ and the full assurance that can result from this exercise.

2 Peter 1:10-11   "Therefore, my brothers, be all the more eager to make your calling and election sure. For if you do these things, you will never fall, and you will receive a rich welcome into the eternal kingdom of our Lord and Savior Jesus Christ." (NIV)

2 Corinthians 13:5   "Examine yourselves to see whether you are in the faith; test yourselves. Do you not realize that Christ Jesus is in you — unless, of course, you fail the test?" (NIV)

Hebrews 6:11-12   "And we desire that every one of you do shew the same diligence to the full assurance of hope unto the end: That ye be not slothful, but followers of them who through faith and patience inherit the promises."

Hebrews 10:21-22   "And since we have a great priest over the house of God, let us draw near with a true heart in full assurance of faith, with our hearts sprinkled clean from an

evil conscience and our bodies washed with pure water."
(RSV)

Colossians 2:1-3   "Let me tell you how hard I have worked
for you and for the people in Laodicea and for all others who do
not know me personally. I do this in order that they may be
filled with courage and may be drawn together in love, and so
have the full wealth of assurance which true understanding
brings. In this way they will know God's secret which is Chris-
thimself." (TEV)

1 Thessalonians 1:5   "For we brought the Good News to
you, not with words only, but also with power and the Holy
Spirit, and with complete conviction of its truth." (TEV)

A sign of development in the young adult age group is their
questioning critically their beliefs and reevaluating their convictions. The intellectual capacity of the young adult is keen.
They are sharp for learning. Consequently they are asking the
kinds of questions which lie beneath other questions. So to
speak, they are "sounding the basis" of their faith in the areas
of salvation, commitment, beliefs and world-life view.

Some of the questions asked by young adults during this
phase of life are: What will I believe about the Lord and about
life? Is Church the right thing for me? These questions relate
to the young adult continuing in the Christian faith?

Those who lead young adults should ask themselves the following kinds of questions about their students: Does the young
adult think that he has outgrown the Church? Is the Church
meeting the needs of the young adult? What kind of place/
future involvement does the young adult envision in the
Church? Is the Christian faith genuine to the young adult? Is
Jesus the only way, or does the young adult feel there are other
ways to get to God? In the eyes of the young adult, how relevant is Christianity to the struggle of Blacks?

Under Aim 5 (below) we discuss the importance of the young
adult learning to effectively study the Word so as to glean
from it both truths that will aid them in understanding life,
and principles by which they can live. Moreover, their learning
to lean on the Holy Spirit is a must if they are to emerge
stronger Christians from the experience of intellectually

examining the faith.

The leaders of young adults should be prayerful, consultative and careful when supporting them in reaching a full assurance in the faith. Unlike Uzzah who sought to steady the consecrated ark of God (2 Samuel 6:6-7), young adult leaders must be careful not to interfere with the consecrated and jealous work of God the Holy Spirit as He transforms the life of the young adult.

Young adults can emerge into some of the best advocates of the Christian faith. But they will not promote their faith unless they see its consistency and believe in its integrity.

(c) Concerning Aim 3:
Mature wholistically, be assured in God's will

Examine the following passages for insights related to the various aspects of the aim.

The next two passages teach us about the will of God.

Colossians 4:12   "Epaphras, who is one of yourselves, a servant of Christ Jesus, greets you, always remembering you earnestly in his prayers, that you may stand mature and fully assured in all the will of God." (RSV)

Ephesians 2:10   "For we are God's workmanship, created in Christ Jesus to do good works, which God prepared in advance for us to do." (NIV)

Ephesians 5:15-17   "Be very careful, then, how you live — not as unwise but as wise, making the most of every opportunity, because the days are evil. Therefore do not be foolish, but understand what the Lord's will is." (NIV)

Following are some of the areas in which a young adult will have to make choices and follow a course of life or action.

1) Who will I be? This is the question of identity. How will the young adult define himself/herself? Will he/she take into consideration his/her Black ethnic and historical roots, or will he/she circumscribe himself/herself to being an "individual," or just a good "American?"

2) What will I be? / What will I do? This is the question of career/occupation/vocation. To what life work will the young adult commit himself? In what areas is he educated, skilled,

gifted? What positions of employment are currently available? Are they "dead end" positions? Should the young adult be concerned with doing some kind of work that will benefit Black people?

3) How should I continue preparing myself? This is the question of continuing education. Which college should the young adult attend? Is it absolutely necessary for him to attend undergraduate, graduate school? What kind of opportunities for continuing education are associated with any given career/occupation? The military?

4) What should I look for in a man/woman? This is the question of courtship-marriage. Who and where are the available Black men/Black women? What kinds of things should the young adult keep in mind when dating/preparing to marry? Should the young adult seek marriage right now or should he/she wait to a later time? Though single, should the young adult woman seek to have a child? Being married, should young adults have children early on or put it off until later?

5) What can I do for fun and relaxation? This is the question of entertainment. In what kinds of activities should the young adult be involved? What kinds of things are acceptable activities for adolescents, but are no longer acceptable for young adults?

The attitude of many Black young adults is "use me or loose me." Recognizing this attitude is important if we are to secure the allegiance of young adults to the Church and to their own people.

Primarily, the Church should communicate to young adults how much it values their membership and begin to include them in the vision and program of the Church. Seek to involve the young adults at every level of the Church's program. Also, those young adults whose lives evidence they are emerging into strong Christian leaders should be placed in the leadership-tracks so that they can ascend into positions of responsibility and service.

Emergent young adults should also be appraised of the crucial role they stand to play in the struggles of Black Americans for complete liberation in this country. Root them in their historical identity. Channel them into studying their history. Spur them to think about creative community programs. Secure their love and commitment to serve their people, and warn them that God does hold them accountable for such service.

(d) Concerning Aim 4:
Depend on the Holy Spirit, appropriate the Word

Consider the following Scriptural passages as they have a bearing on the Holy Spirit, the Word of God, and maturity.

Hebrews 5:12-6:1   "In fact, though by this time you ought to be teachers, you need someone to teach you the elementary truths of God's word all over again. You need milk, not solid food! Anyone who lives on milk, being still an infant, is not acquainted with the teaching about righteousness. But solid food is for the mature, who by constant use have trained themselves to distinguish good from evil. Therefore let us leave the elementary teachings about Christ and go on to maturity..." (NIV).

2 Timothy 3:16   "All Scripture is God-breathed and is useful for teaching, rebuking, correcting and training in righteousness, so that the man of God may be thoroughly equipped for every good work." (NIV)

John 14:26   "But the Counselor, the Holy Spirit, whom the Father will send in my name, will teach you all things and will remind you of everything I [Jesus] have said to you." (NIV)

John 16:13a   "But when he, the Spirit of truth, comes, he will guide you into all truth." (NIV)

1 John 2:20   "But you have an anointing from the Holy One, and all of you know the truth." (NIV)

1 John 2:26-27   "As for you, the anointing you received from him remains in you, and you do not need anyone to teach you. But as his anointing teaches you about all things and as that anointing is real, not counterfeit — just as it has taught you, remain in him." (NIV)

This area of development in the life of the young adult is

most crucial. For being successful in achieving the other aims will depend on how well this one is accomplished. Just as all other Christians, the emergent young adult must learn to depend on the Holy Spirit and appropriate the Word. This is the way to maturity for each Christian young adult.

The emergent young adult should be taught how to effectively study the Scripture. It is one thing to be taught the Word, but it is quite another thing to know how to teach oneself the Word. The Christian young adult can be taught various biblical study methods. And generally speaking, he is ready to engage himself in a disciplined study of the Word.

Two avenues for helping the young adult learn how to study the Scriptures are through books and special biblical courses. Each Church should have a body of simple "how to study the Bible" books available for its young adults. The young adult is a reader. His mental capacities are rapidly developing. He can absorb much information. This is why he should be provided with a good diet of biblical literature that will help him develop his biblical study skills. Also, the Christian young adult should be provided with the kinds of books which highlight the world of the Bible. Understanding the cultures, history, people, places, geography, etc., of the Bible will greatly enhance the young adult's development.

Every now and then the young adults should be provided with some kind of an "elective" course, either in conjunction with the Sunday School, the Church's training hour, or some other program. The purpose of such a course should not so much be to teach the lesson, but to help the young adults learn the lesson for themselves. Following is a simple Bible study guide that was used in this way with a group of young adults.

* * * * * * * * * * * *

Young Adult Bible Study Guide

Aim:

To learn about biblical persons who, because they had a good relationship with the Lord, were concerned for the survival of their people as they lived among other nations. This is done with a view toward our becoming likewise more concerned for the survival of our people in this nation in the name of the Lord.

Persons we will study:
Moses, Esther, Nehemiah, Daniel

(Divide the young adults into study groups of three to five persons each. Each study group will examine the life of one person. The teacher should provide Scriptural/historical background information for each person to be studied.)

Scripture to read:
1. Moses: Exodus 2:1-3:12; Acts 7:17-38; Hebrews 11:23-29
2. Esther: Esther 3:7-4:17; 7:1-8:6ff.
3. Nehemiah: Nehemiah 1:1-2:20; 4:1-5:19
4. Daniel: Daniel 1:1-21

Questions for study groups:

1. Describe the nation the Israelite/Jewish people were living among?
2. What was the problem, kind of oppression they were experiencing?
3. How do we recognize the commitment of these "deliverers" to God?
4. What kinds of alternatives could these chosen instruments of God have opted for rather than take the course of action which they did?
5. How do we know the people were ready for deliverance?
6. How were the people delivered from the oppression?
7. What kinds of parallels do we see in our own lives?
8. Was there a key verse in your passage that seemed to unlock the story?

* * * * * * * * * * * * * *

The emergent young adult also needs the power and ministry of the Holy Spirit in his life. The Holy Spirit is the One who will help the young adult understand the Word. He will also help the young adult apply the Word to his life. Then too, the Holy Spirit is the One who will help the believing young adult to mature as a Christian. The young adult must depend on the Holy Spirit.

There is a lot of talk about "spirituality" among young adult circles. The careful listener will discern that not all people talking about spirituality are saying nor meaning the same thing. The young adult needs direction in this area. He needs a proper understanding of the Person and work of the Holy Spirit if he would rightly depend on Him. The Church which is serious about its ministry to young adults will spend time teaching them about the Spirit of God. (See appendix for a brief biblical study of Christian spirituality.)

(e) Concerning Aim 5:
Settle into adulthood, serve Christ and people

Read the following verses which speak to the young adult becoming settled into fully serving Christ.

Matthew 6:25, 31-34 "Therefore I tell you, do not be anxious about your life, what you shall eat or what you shall drink, nor about your body, what you shall put on. Is not life more than food, and the body more than clothing?...Therefore do not be anxious, saying, 'What shall we eat?' or 'What shall we drink?' or 'What shall we wear?' For the Gentiles seek all these things; and your heavenly Father knows that you need them all. But seek first his kingdom and his righteousness, and all these things shall be yours as well. Therefore do not be anxious about tomorrow, for tomorrow will be anxious for itself. Let the day's own trouble be sufficient for the day." (RSV)

1 Corinthians 7:26-32, 35   "Because of the present crisis, I think that it is good for you to remain as your are. Are you married? Do not seek a divorce. Are you unmarried? Do not look for a wife. But if you do marry, you have not sinned; and if a virgin marries, she has not sinned. But those who marry will face many troubles in this life, and I want to spare you this. What I mean, brothers, is that the time is short. From now on those who have wives should live as if they had none; those who mourn, as if they did not; those who are happy, as if they were not; those who buy something, as if it were not theirs to

keep; those who use the things of the world, as if not engrossed in them. For this world in its present form is passing away. I would like you to be free from concern...I am saying this for your own good, not to restrict you, but that you may live in a right way in undivided devotion to the Lord." (NIV)

1 Corinthians 10:31   "So, whether you eat or drink, or whatever you do, do all to the glory of God." (RSV)

The important point to remember for the fifth aim is that young adults need to become settled as middle adults. In doing so they need to pursue courses of life that do not detract them from giving full, wholehearted service to the Lord. Young adults are prone toward materialistic values and pursuits, and many have the money to support the habit. Also, they can become overly active and busy, leaving little time in a crowded schedule for spiritual matters, both personal and in the Church.

Young adults can become pre-occupied with their occupations and careers, and even become burdened down with life's responsibilities. This pre-occupation can become a great hindrance to the young adult's spiritual development and the dedicated service he should give to Christ. This is especially the case for the young adult who does not view his career/occupation as an avenue for bringing the presence and claims of Christ to bear upon the world.

Nothing should hinder the young adult from serving Christ. Whether it is securing life-sustaining food and drink, or getting clothing for the body; whether it is worries about the troubles of the present day or the troubles of tomorrow; whether it is marriage, singleness, death, celebration, purchasing, or just plain using available resources — nothing, absolutely nothing should distract the young adult from serving the Lord Christ.

When Black young adults reach full adulthood, they should be free to work, build, and exert their power and influence for Christ. They should know clearly what they are all about so that they can immerse themselves in their work for Christ, especially as this work relates to serving Black people. Whatever the cost, they should avoid taking on the encumbrances associated with making a living and with life itself. The Black young adult who remembers the words Paul wrote to young adult Timothy will do himself well: "No soldier on service gets entangled in civilian pursuits, since his aim is to satisfy the one who enlisted him" (2 Timothy 2:4, RSV).

3. Programming the aims

The objective for teaching Christian Black young adults and its five aims need to be broken down into attainable steps so that they can be reached by each young adult and measured by young adult leaders. This process will require some thinking and planning, but it should not be too difficult for the Sunday School superintendent, young adult leaders, or the director of Christian education to do. Enlist the assistance of someone in the Church who is gifted at conceptualizing and writing.

Once the objective and its aims have been structured to cover most aspects of life related to young adults, these areas can then be placed into the over all program of the Church as it relates to ministering to its young adults. This is important. For if these precepts are not set in place, they will probably not be reached.

Different auxiliaries of the Church can be assigned the task of overseeing specific aspects of the young adult curriculum. The Sunday School, the young adult fellowship group, the training arm of the Church, etc. — each will have a role to play in developing the emerging young adult. Just make sure the work is being done. The future of the Church and survival and well-being of Black America is at stake.

Chapter 9

Teaching Black Young Adults in the Sunday School

A. Rethinking Our Approach

Before proceeding any further, it is time for us to step back and rethink the manner in which Black young adults are taught. This is important for two reasons. One, young adults should not be taught as one teaches Black children. Unlike some children, the "obedience to elders" appeal is not suitable for young adults. Neither can the instructor circumscribe the experiences of young adults as a parent or guardian might be able to do for a child.

Two, young adults should not be taught as some teachers try to teach young people: by brow-beating them and intimidation, if not, by "preaching" them down into outward and shallow submission. Black young adults know too much and are too matured to continually put up with such non-sense. They will not be controlled in ways like some teachers control ("manipulate") children and young people.

The teaching ministry among young adults deserves a more open approach. Toward this end we offer the following piece. It first appeared in the inaugural edition of Urban Outreach's new Sunday School publication for those persons 17/18 years and above, and is named *Young Adult TODAY.* The article provided young adult instructors an understanding of the literature, showing them how best to use the material. Thus, *it is an explanation of the purpose of* **Young Adult TODAY** *in the context of strengthening the teacher and improving the learning sessions of young adults.* This thought should be kept in mind as the article is being read.

B. A Model —
Teaching Young Adults Using
Young Adult TODAY

1. The Aim of *Young Adult TODAY*

Those persons who worked in developing *TODAY* and *TODAY Leader* did so with a special aim in mind.

(a) The purpose of TODAY and TODAY Leader is to develop, through the Church's Sunday School, mature and fulfilled Christ-centered young adults by motivating biblical discussion centered around the needs and critical issues facing Black American young adults.

(b) The discussion should be conducted with a view toward their both gaining an understanding of related biblical principles and being guided in making responsible personal and social life applications of these principles.

(c) The understanding and application of these biblical principles is intended to be fostered under the direction of (1) provocative lessons, (2) discussion oriented class-sessions, and (3) knowledgeable and emotionally mature teachers educated in the teaching-style of motivating and educating students through self-directed and supervised learning.

2. An Explanation of our Aim

(a) To develop Christ-centered young adults through pertinent biblical discussion

Through *TODAY* and *TODAY Leader* we desire to develop mature and fulfilled Black young adults who have Christ as the center of their lives. Christ is all, and we want Him to become everything to young adults. We assume that the young adults being taught already have a saving knowledge of the Lord Jesus Christ. Therefore, evangelism is not our main purpose, though it should become apparent that in the course of using the materials the teacher will see natural applications for the unsaved. The lost will be challenged with the redemptive claims of Christ Jesus.

We feel a key to developing such young adults will lie in our ability to engage them in lively *discussion*. Young adults can not and should not be taught as though they were children. They have arrived at the age, and should manifest a certain degree of maturity, to carry on a meaningful discussion around the Bible.

In the context of the Bible, young adult Black Christians should discuss issues and needs relevant to themselves as Black American Christians. *TODAY* and *TODAY Leader* are intended to be close to the heartbeat of "what's happening," particularly with Black young adults. We desire to address them exactly where they are, and not five years later! We want the publications to be socially timely.

(b) To help them understand biblical principles and make responsible applications

What do we envision accomplishing in the lives of young adults through discussion? Two things: their acquiring an understanding of *biblical principles*, and their making responsible life *applications* of these principles.

Young adults should have moved passed the stage of learning isolated and apparently unrelated Bible verses. Instead, they should become aware of essential biblical principles which impact their general knowledge about life and their way of living. As revealed throughout His Word, we want our young adults to grasp the ways and patterns of God as He relates to His creatures. The coherency of thought in the Christian faith should become evident to young adults.

Close on the heals of understanding biblical principles is the work of *applying* them. We desire to guide our young adults through to the application phase of Christian growth. We believe that faith without obedient action is dead. Likewise will become the young adult who knows all the right things but fails to put them into practice.

TODAY and *TODAY Leader* encourage both personal and social applications. In no way do we desire to Christianly educate persons who turn out to be "Christians unto themselves." Our aim is to maturate Black young adult Christians who, building on their personal growth in Christ, see the value of giving social expression to their faith. Our hope is that the presence of godly young adults will affect their generation and their society for Christ.

(c) To achieve the optimum benefits from the learning situation
(1) Provocative lessons
The lessons in *TODAY* and *TODAY Leader* are written in a tone that is *provocative*. This tone seems best fitted to generate discussion, provoking young adults to think about the topic under consideration. This tone also serves as a prod useful for arousing young adults to action. Like avoiding the plague, we will strenuously guard against the kind of written style that would dull the intellectual and spiritual senses of young adults and lull them into apathy; especially when a major characteristic their age-group should manifest is a social action orientation.

(2) Discussion oriented class sessions
The provocative lessons in the publications are not

87

intended, however, to become platforms for teachers to lecture and "preach" during the Sunday School hour. The lessons are not geared for class sessions that turn out to be monologues by the instructor. We look for dialog and the form of discussion wherein the flow of conversation not only travels back and forth from teacher to student, but also travels back and forth between student and student. This is effective group discussion.

(3) Competent teachers

So, what quality of teacher do we best think can do the above? We answer, those teachers who themselves are maturing in their relationship with the Lord Christ, who are both *knowledgeable and emotionally mature*.

TODAY and *TODAY Leader* are waiting to be used by teachers who are growing in knowledge and understanding. This includes a broad knowledge of life as well as a good knowledge of the Word of God. Today's Black Christian young adults are quick to perceive and point out when their "teachers" are unprepared, mis-informed, and shallow in presentation. They want and need substance; instructors who know, and who know they know what they are talking about. At the least, young adults need leaders who are committed to searching out and uncovering answers for questions which they themselves and their class raise.

Now in order to lead the kinds of provocative discussions we envision, it it most important that the instructor be *emotionally mature*. Those who teach young adults should be prepared to discuss most anything. They must be able to handle the "heat" of the classroom kitchen.

Also, the teacher's emotional state should be such that he responds in a mature fashion to students who expose themselves (and expose their instructors!) in the normal process of discussion and learning. Without question, such an instructor must exhibit gifts associated with counseling and personally carry himself in such a manner that the students feel comfortable in approaching him for personal counsel.

Finally, the instructors who teach *TODAY* and *TO-DAY Leader* should learn and cultivate the kind of teaching-style that lends itself to "motivating and educating students through self-directed and supervised learning." The instructor should shy away from telling the class everything: what to believe, how to act, where to go, etc. We want the students to discover the truth and make applications for themselves.

In this sense, the teacher becomes a guide who takes advantage of the motivations expressed by the student and uses them to channel the student in the proper direction. The teacher walks the learner through the process leading to Christ-centered maturity and fulfillment, and challenges the learner to explore and examine other worthy paths along the way.

The instructor of Black young adults who prays, who takes the time and effort, and who pays the price to teach in this wise, will find *TODAY* and *TODAY Leader* most helpful to his teaching ministry and some very exciting publications. And we ask that the young adult instructor will remember to pray for those who contribute to the making of this Black and biblical literature. We want God to get the glory from its pages.

* * * * * * * * * *

3. The intended message

Obviously, the preceding section dealt with teaching Black young adults in the Church's Sunday School. In a way this emphasis is good because most of the teaching done in our churches occurs during the Sunday School hour. However, the principles discussed are applicable to teaching young adults in other contexts as well. (We would hope, as a result of this discussion, that some of our churches would be inspired to start special programs for their young adults so that they can receive time for additional teaching and activities centered around their needs and potential.)

With a birds-eye view, let us briefly list some of the important things to nurture when engaging in a teaching ministry for Black young adults.

(a) The Message for young adults

1. Young adults should become mature and fulfilled, through their lives becoming Christ-centered.

2. Young adults should engage themselves in lively biblical discussion.

3. Young adults should discuss their needs and critical issues facing them as Black Americans.

4. Young adults should learn biblical principles rather than just isolated and apparently unrelated Bible verses.

5. Young adults should be guided in making responsible personal and social applications of the Word.

6. Young adults should be taught lessons that are provocative in tone.

7. Young adults should not be "preached" to during the class session but taught through the method of discussion and dialog.

(b) The message for young adult teachers

1. Young adult teachers should submit their teaching to an aim which is geared toward effectively ministering to their students.

2. Young adult teachers should be maturing in their own relationship with the Lord, becoming both knowledgeable and emotionally mature.

3. Young adult teachers should have the gifts and demeanor that befit those who are counselors.

4. Young adult teachers should possess the kind of teaching-style of a guide who motivates and helps students discover and apply for themselves what they learn.

5. Young adult teachers should pray, take the time and effort, and pay the price to teach Black young adults effectively.

4. A teaching plan for young adults

Following is a brief teaching plan which we find useful when teaching young adults.

(a) Questions motivating discussion

The teacher should formulate as many questions as possible. The purpose of these questions is to motivate discussion among the students. It is not necessary to attempt to get the students to answer all the questions at the start of the lesson. Actually, these questions should be interspersed throughout the learning session. Discussion should flow through most of the period.

(b) Whetting the appetite

This aspect of the teaching plan serves as the attention grabber. It is introduced on a level which strikes a cord in the students' experiences. Perhaps it focuses on one of their felt needs, or picks up on one of the hot topics being discussed in their circle. In whatever manner it is introduced, its purpose is to get the attention of the students so that their minds are thinking in the same direction.

(c) Spotlighting the issue/need

As the lesson progresses, this phase will serve the purpose of narrowing the topic which the class must handle for the day. For instance, if the subject raised above is "careers," then this section would focus the topic of discussion around, for example, "understanding God's will as it relates to our careers." Further, the students are brought into an awareness that they cannot afford to miss the truths that will be communicated through discussing this particular topic.

(d) Conveying the biblical principle

This is the "meat" of the class session. The students must be brought to an understanding that the Word of God speaks to the topic at hand. Carefully they must be guided into discovering for themselves the principles related to this area of life.

Therefore, the teacher must make certain that his explanation of the Scripture is clear and indeed rooted in the passage under consideration. The students may also suggest other verses which have a bearing on the topic. This is good and approaches the ideal learning situation for young adults.

(e) Guiding the application

The goal of the class is not to merely discuss the Word, but also to apply it. The instructor should avoid telling the students what to do (unless absolutely necessary). Instead, suggest a few ways the biblical principles that were discovered are capable of being applied to their lives. Trust the Holy Spirit to teach the students what they should be doing as a result of what they have learned. Some times it is good to close the class session without "closing" the class session. In other words, every now and then leave something to think about on the minds of the students. Let them wrestle with the issues. Their lives will turn out better as a result of the process.

Chapter 10

Helping the Emerging Black Young Adult to Emerge

A. A Crucial Time

For the teacher who has success in teaching young adults, part of this success will be attributable to how effectively he helps the young adult understand his point of growth in the maturation process. That is, in order to be effectively taught, the young adult should possess an accurate perception of his own growth. (This relates to the volitional characteristic ofemerging young adults as discussed earlier.)

At one point or another parents with young people are confronted with the young person who desires, begs, or demands to be treated as an "adult." The same also happens with those who teach young adults. When this time does arrive, it is important that whoever is in the superior role (parent, guardian, teacher, pastor) handle the situation properly.

At this point we can return to the first part of this study covering Understanding Black Young Adults. In this section we were provided with nine signs of maturity which become criteria for recognizing an emergent Black young adult. In other words, the following can become a sort of "test," determining to what degree a young person is becoming a young adult.

B. A Test of Emergent Black Young Adulthood

1. I am a young adult because I have taken steps to move away from economical dependence on my parents to providing my own economic base.
Yes   No   Partially

2. I am a young adult because I have consciously made the determination to define myself as an adult and decisively have resolved and chosen to begin living like a young adult, not like an adolescent.
Yes   No   Not quite

3. I am a young adult because I am recognized and affirmed as an adult by a representative cross-section of the older adults with whom I come into contact.
Yes   No   About 50%

4. I am a young adult because I am becoming increasingly responsible for making my own decisions and for establishing my own actions and behavior.
Yes   No   Most decisions

5. I am a young adult because I show maturity in accepting the full consequences of my own decisions and actions.
Yes   No   Sometimes

6. I am a young adult because in many areas of life I have clearly decided what my values are and am following a course of life this is consistent with them.
Yes   No   Some of my values

7. I am a young adult because I am making my presence

felt in a responsible manner in my community for its betterment.

Yes   No   Not involved

8. I am a young adult because I both understand and, of my own determination, have actively committed myself to a process of emergence into maturity.

Yes   No   Still sort of floating

9. I am a young adult because I have attained a full assurance of faith in the Lord Christ Jesus and am "coming into my own in the Lord."

Yes   No   My life is partially committed

The quest for a young person to be treated as a young adult can be used as a situation of learning and growth. When the young person begins to perceive the areas in which he/she needs to mature, then he/she can be channeled and challenged in those directions, and his/her progress can be measured.

Remember, teaching young adults involves more than disseminating information. It also covers developing them in terms of their potential.

C. Scriptural Considerations Applicable to Emergence

1. Economically, independent

"But we exhort you, brethren, to do so more and more, to aspire to live quietly, to mind your own affairs, and to work with your hands, as we charged you; so that you may command the respect of outsiders, and be dependent on nobody" (1 Thessalonians 4:10b-12, RSV).

Notice in this passage a command to be dependent on nobody.

"For even when we were with you, we gave you this command: If any one will not work, let him not eat. For we hear that some of you are living in idleness, mere busybodies, not doing any work. Now such persons we command and exhort in the Lord Jesus Christ to do their work in quietness and to earn their own living. Brethren, do not be weary in well-doing" (2 Thessalonians 3:10-13, RSV)

Notice in this passage the contrast between idleness and work, and the command for each person to earn his own living.

2. Psychologically, self-defined

"When David's time to die drew near, he charged Solomon his son, saying, 'I am about to go the way of all the earth. Be strong, and show yourself a man, and keep the charge of the Lord your God, walking in his ways and keeping his statues, his commandments, his ordinances, and his testimonies, as it is written in the law of Moses, that you may prosper in all that you do and wherever you turn' " (1 Kings 2:1-3, RSV).

Notice in this passage how David told Solomon his son to show himself a man.

"Don't let anyone look down on you because you are young, but set an example for the believers in speech, in life, in love, in faith and in purity" (1 Timothy 4:12, NIV).

Notice in this passage how the young man Timothy is told to model a new character so that his young-adultness would have a redefinition (he was around 30 at the time).

3. Socially, affirmed by older adults

"His parents answered, 'We know that this is our son, and that he was born blind; but how he now sees we do not know, nor do we know who opened his eyes. Ask him; he is of age, he will speak for himself' " (John 9:20-21, RSV).

Notice in this passage how the man's parents recognized his maturity and gave him space to exercise it (even though they did it to save their own necks! cf. John 9:22-23).

4. Accountability-wise, responsible for own decisions

"Jephthah answered, 'I and my people were engaged in a great struggle with the Ammonites, and although I called, you didn't save me out of their hands. When I saw that you wouldn't help, I took my life in my hands and crossed over to fight the Ammonites, and the Lord gave me the victory over them' " (Judges 12:2-3a, NIV).

Notice in this passage how Jephthah takes charge of his own life and well-being by resolving what to do and doing it.

"Take courage, and acquit yourselves like men, O Philistines, lest you become slaves to the Hebrews as they have been to you; acquit yourselves like men and fight" (1 Samuel 4:9, RSV).

Notice in this passage the determination of the Philistines to fight for their freedom as a manifestation of their manhood.

5. Emotionally, accepting consequences of actions

"I will arise and go to my father, and I will say to him, 'Father, I have sinned against heaven and before you; I am no longer worthy to be called your son; treat me as one of your hired servants' " (Luke 15:18-19, RSV).

Notice from this passage the "blame-nobody-but-myself" attitude of this son who made some bad decisions, suffered for it, and sought help from his father.

"Go, gather all the Jews to be found in Susa, and hold a fast on my behalf, and neither eat nor drink for three days, night or day. I and my maids will also fast as you do. Then I will go to the king, though it is against the law; and if I perish, I perish" (Esther 4:16, RSV).

Notice in this passage the "if-it-doesn't-work-out-I-am-prepared-to-suffer-the-consequences" attitude of Queen Esther.

6. Value-wise, settling of values

"When I was a child, I spoke like a child, I thought like a child, I reasoned like a child; when I became a man, I gave up childish ways" (1 Corinthians 13:11, RSV).

Notice in this passage the three areas of maturity for the young adult: communication, attitude, and reasoning; and the break with childish ways.

"Brothers, stop thinking like children. In regard to evil be infants, but in your thinking be adults" (1 Corinthians 14:20, NIV).

Notice in this passage the call to think like an adult and to engage oneself in positive values.

7. Community-wise, involved in development
"This is a trustworthy saying. And I want you to stress these things, so that those who have trusted in God may be careful to devote themselves to doing what is good. These things are excellent and profitable for everyone" (Titus 3:8, NIV).

Notice in this passage the call for community involvement (cf. vv. 1-8).

"Be of good courage, and let us play the man for our people, and for the cities of our God; and may the Lord do what seems good to him" (2 Samuel 10:12, RSV).

Notice in this passage the correlation between manhood and protecting one's people and one's community.

8. Volitionally, committed to emergence
"By faith Moses, when he was grown up, refused to be called the son of Pharaoh's daughter, choosing rather to share ill-treatment with the people of God than to enjoy the fleeting pleasures of sin. He considered abuse suffered for the Christ greater wealth than the treasures of Egypt, for he looked to the reward" (Hebrews 11:24-26, RSV).

Notice in this passage the association of the "grown up"-ness of Moses with his self-determination to suffer and grow thereby.

"'Look,' said Naomi, 'your sister-in-law is going back to her people and her gods. Go back with her.'" But Ruth replied, 'Don't urge me to leave you or to turn back from you. Where you go I will go, and where you stay I will stay. Your people will be my people and your God my God. Where you die I will die, and there I will be buried. May the Lord deal with me, be it ever so severely, if anything but death separates you and me.' When Naomi realized that Ruth was determined to go with her, she stopped urging her" (Ruth 1:15-18, NIV).

Notice in this passage the self-motivated commitment of

Ruth to a process of emergence that would call for major changes in her life.

"And he went down with them and came to Nazareth, and was obedient to them; and his mother kept all these things in her heart. And Jesus increased in wisdom and in stature, and in favor with God and man" (Luke 2:51-52, RSV).

Notice in this passage the willing obedience/subjection of Jesus to his parents and his subsequent wholistic growth.

9. Spiritually, attaining full assurance in the faith

"And He said to them, 'Why is it that you sought Me? Did you not know that I must be about My Father's business?'" (Luke 2:49, NKJV).

Notice in this passage how Jesus has "come into his own" in His relationship with His Father. Notice His confidence and resolve.

"Now Thomas, one of the twelve, called the Twin, was not with them when Jesus came. So the other disciples told him, 'We have seen the Lord.' But he said to them, 'Unless I see in his hands the print of the nails, and place my finger in the mark of the nails, and place my hand in his side, I will not believe.' Eight days later, his disciples were again in the house, and Thomas was with them. The doors were shut, but Jesus came and stood among them, and said, 'Peace be with you.' Then he said to Thomas, 'Put your finger here, and see my hands; and put out your hand, and place it in my side; do not be faithless, but believing.' Thomas answered him, 'My Lord and my God!' Jesus said to him, 'Have you believed because you have seen me? Blessed are those who have not seen and yet believe'" (John 20:24-29, RSV).

Notice in this passage the concern of Jesus for "doubting" Thomas, and the reaffirmation of Thomas's faith in the Lord after examination of the evidence.

D. Working Toward Accomplishment

It is recommended that these nine dimensions of growth for young adults be accomplished as early as possible in their lives. We believe that it is feasible for a Black young adult to have attained these standards of progress by the time he reaches age 23 or 24. Then, from age 25-34 the emergent young adult should be concentrating on acquiring those qualities of life that will prepare him for entering into Christ-centered middle adulthood.

These nine dimensions can be achieved step by step by each young person until they are all fulfilled. It is not necessary, however, to follow the order in which they are listed here. For example, one creative way of accomplishing the nine might be:

> *First, accountability-wise*
> *Second, emotionally*
> *Third, value-wise*
> *Fourth, volitionally*
> *Fifth, psychologically*
> *Sixth, economically*
> *Seventh, socially affirmed*
> *Eighth, spiritually*
> *Ninth, community-wise*

The order in which one approaches these steps of maturation may or may not be important, depending on the circumstances. And there will be some overlap between different areas. The key is to make certain that all are being accomplished in the life of the emergent young adult.

It is primarily the role of the parents to oversee the growth of their young people into full young adulthood. This is their God-given privilege and responsibility. The Scripture teaches: "And you, fathers, do not provoke your children to wrath, but bring them up in the training and admonition of the Lord" (Ephesians 6:4, NKJV).

Secondarily, it is the leadership of Christian young adults who should commit themselves to helping each young adult in the Church fulfill these areas of growth. Whatever time and kinds of resources it takes, it is imperative that the leadership within the Black Church bring its Black young adults into their complete emergence. The Church needs mature Black young adults and so do Black people. Moreover, it is personally beneficial for each young adult to be mature.

100

Chapter 11

Empowering and Equipping Black Young Adults to Strengthen the Church through Spiritual Gifts

A. Strengthen through Spiritual Gifts

A primary way that Black young adults can strengthen the Church is through their use of spiritual gifts. For it will be through the exercising of their spiritual gifts that young adults will find their proper place in the Body. Someone has said, "When people know and use their spiritual gifts there is no need for them to fight over 'positions' in the Church." How true. If each Church member properly used his gift(s), there would not be so much fussing and fighting and jockeying for positions of prestige and power in our local congregations.

It is the responsibility of the Church to empower and to equip its members for service to the Body of Christ (as well as to the community). This can be done through bringing the believers into a good understanding of spiritual gifts. Yet, the area of spiritual gifts is an area of serious neglect in the ministry of the Church to Black young adults. And little wonder, for many of our congregations, not just our young adults, are totally or minimally aware of biblical teaching about spiritual gifts.

Through teaching and experience we have learned that many young adults become excited as they learn about the work of the Holy Spirit in bestowing spiritual gifts on all God's children. Furthermore, they are overcome with a sense of fulfillment and satisfaction when they learn which gifts have been given them by the Lord.

B. The Importance of Emphasizing Spiritual Gifts

The importance of bringing young adults into an awareness of spiritual gifts cannot be minimized. For one thing, it highlights the work of God the Holy Spirit as One Who is not just around to make Christians "feel good" or "have a good time." The Spirit of God is the One Who, through His gifts, personally strengthens each believer, and equips each for doing a special service in the Church and in the world.

Second, the Holy Spirit is the One who controls the Church and causes it to function as the body of Christ in the world. And the main way the Spirit of God does this work is through persons who are filled with the Spirit and use the gifts which are given by Him.

Third, in a very real sense, the gifts of the Holy Spirit give each Christian a special place and role to fulfill in the Church. This means that each young adult can be meaningfully involved in the work of the Church. As Solomon said, "A man's gift makes room for him and brings him before great men" (Proverbs 18:16, RSV).

C. Understanding Spiritual Gifts

We think it is good for us to provide you with a small amount of teaching about Spiritual gifts, even though space does not permit a more exhaustive treatment. So let us consider several Bible passages which highlight spiritual gifts.

1. A biblical division of gifts

1 Corinthians 12:4-6 — "Now there are varieties of gifts, but the same Spirit; and there are varieties of service, but the same Lord; and there are varieties of working, but it is the same God who inspires them all in every one" (RSV).

This verse shows a three-fold division of spiritual gifts into 1) gifts (gifts of grace, charismata); 2) services and 3) workings.

2. Gifts of grace

Romans 12:6-8 — "Having then gifts differing according to the grace that is given to us, whether prophecy, let us prophesy according to the proportion of faith; or ministry, let us wait on our ministering; or he that teacheth, on teaching; Or he that exhorteth, on exhortation: he that giveth, let him do it with simplicity; he that ruleth, with diligence; he that sheweth mercy, with cheerfulness."

It appears that God gives one of these seven gifts of grace to each believer. For the word commands each Christian to "wait," that is to concentrate on his gift. And a person can concentrate on but one thing at a time. Each gift of grace is like a "charisma" bestowed on each believer. When a Christian exercises his own gift of grace, there will be a great freedom in his life and others will be attracted to him. For the exercising of the gift will become obviously effective.

3. Services

Ephesians 4:7-13 — "But to each one of us grace has been given as Christ apportioned it. This is why it says: 'When he ascended on high, he led captives in his train and gave gifts to men.' (What does 'he ascended' mean except that he also descended to the lower, earthly regions? He who descended is the very one who ascended higher than all the heavens, in order to fill the whole universe.) It was he who gave some to be apostles, some to be prophets, some to be evangelists, and some to be pastors and teachers, to prepare God's people for works of service, so that the body of Christ may be built up until we all reach unity in the faith and in the knowledge of the Son of God and become mature, attaining to the whole measure of the fullness of Christ" (NIV).

1 Corinthians 12:28-31 — "And God hath set some in the church, first apostles, secondarily prophets, thirdly teachers, after that miracles, then gifts of healings, helps, governments, diversities of tongues. Are all apostles? are all prophets? are all teachers? are all workers of miracles? Have all the gifts of healing? do all speak with tongues? do all interpret? But covet earnestly the best gifts: and yet shew I unto you a more excellent way."

One should notice that these gifts (services) are not what the people possess but who they are. Christ gives people as *service-gifts* to the Church. That is, each believer is himself a gift to the Church from Christ. Christ "sets" or appoints them in the Church.

It is good for the young adults in the Church to understand these service-gifts especially. For the using of these gifts will move them directly into areas of service in the Church. They will be able to function in the Church with a greater freedom and confidence because they will understand their place.

4. Workings

1 Corinthians 12:7-11 — "To each is given the manifestation of the Spirit for the common good. To one is given through the Spirit the utterance of wisdom, and to another the utterance of knowledge according to the same Spirit, and to another faith by the same Spirit, to another gifts of healing by the one Spirit, to another the working of miracles, to another prophecy, to another the ability to distinguish between spirits, to another various kinds of tongues, to another the interpretation of tongues. All these are inspired by one and the same Spirit, who apportions to each one individually as he wills" (RSV).

Several things can be noted concerning the gifts called "workings." One, the manifestation of the Spirit is given to each Christian for the common good. This means that the gifts may be personal but they are not to be exercised in an individualistical manner. Two, the Spirit bestows these gifts upon each Christian just as He determines. This means that the Spirit of God will give as many of the workings to a believer as

He wills to do so. God the Holy Spirit shows himself sovereign in this matter.

D. A Seminar or Weekly Sessions on Spiritual Gifts

Below is a schedule for a one-day seminar on Spiritual gifts. It may be adapted to better suit the needs of a particular congregation. We suggest that a Church go into prayer and search for a young adult couple who will give themselves to the study of spiritual gifts and then prepare themselves to share what they learn with other members of the congregation.

* * * * * * * * * * * *

Spiritual Gifts Seminar

8:30 A.M.	Registration
9:00-9:15	Devotional
9:15-9:30	Welcome, Purpose, Overview of Syllabus
9:30-10:00	The Work of the Holy Spirit a) In the Church b) In the Christian c) Through Spiritual Gifts
10:00-10:30	Discovery Groups - I Survey and Reading of Bible Passages related to Spiritual Gifts
10:30-11:30	Understanding Spiritual Gifts - I a) The nature of Spiritual Gifts b) The identification of Spiritual Gifts
11:30-12:00	Question/Answer - Discussion
12:00 NOON	LUNCH & Discovery Groups - II The value of Spiritual Gifts to the Christian
1:00-1:45 P.M.	Understanding Spiritual Gifts - II a) Their inter-relation one to the other b) Guarding against their misuse
1:45-2:15	Discover Groups - III Uncovering your own Spiritual Gifts

2:15-2:55	Understanding Spiritual Gifts - III a) Serving the Church through Spiritual Gifts b) Serving the Community through Spiritual Gifts
2:55-3:00	Closing Remarks, Prayer of Thanksgiving, Benediction

* * * * * * * * * * * * * * *

Initially, some churches may not choose to commence their study of spiritual gifts with a seminar. In this case, a weekly study course may be developed. One of my associates in the ministry (a Rev. Donald Smith, Chicago, IL) conducts such a weekly course. The results have been most rewarding. Session after session young adults (and older adults as well!) testify to having discovered their spiritual gifts through their indepth studies.

Chapter 12

Using Christian Organizations to Further Develop your Young Adults

A. The Need

Sometimes it is necessary for a congregation to look beyond its doors in order to discover what resources are available for continuing the Christian development of their young adults. The leadership of a given congregation may not be properly educated or gifted in order to meet some of the pressing needs of its young adults. The young adult himself may need a broader exposure to the Christian faith that will enable him to properly focus his role in his Church. Whatever the situation, it is good to know about resources which are available to strengthen the local congregation.

B. The Right Kind of Resource Organization

It is wise for a pastor to know what kind of organizations he is dealing with. For not all organizations whose ministries are geared toward reaching Black young adults are equally beneficial to the overall well-being of Black congregations. This is another way of saying that when some organizations have finished "teaching" some Black young adults, the local congregation might as well be "finished" with its young adult! That is, some organizations which minister to Black young adults develop the kind of persons who make life more difficult for the Church rather than help it. Pastor, beware.

We would recommend that Black congregations use the following criteria (or something similar to it) when looking for an organization to strengthen its young adults.

1) Is the leadership of that organization active members of a Church in the Black tradition?

2) Does the leadership of that organization have a healthy respect for the Christian experiences and traditions of Black people?

3) What is the attitude of the organization's leadership to Black leadership as a whole? Black leadership in the Church?

4) Is the philosophy of the organization one which encourages the Black young adult to faithfully work in his Church in a service role?

5) Does the organization encourage Black young adults to live within and build up their community?

6) Will Black Christians be those who teach your young adults, or at the least someone who understands and appreciates the Black experience?

7) Does the organization teach the Bible as the Bible?

These are the kinds of questions Black congregations are encouraged to consider when evaluating the appropriateness of an organization to supplement the Christian education of their young adults. For it does no good for a Church to rear one of its children through adolescence, only to find that in a few months somebody has "poisoned" his mind and spirit against his Church and people.

C. Three Helpful Organizations

The author is familiar with three organizations in the city of Chicago that can help Black churches teach their young adults.

1. Sonlight Productions Youth Ministry

1613 W. Washington Blvd.
Chicago, IL 60612
Founder/Executive Producer: Rev. Michael Walton
(312) 733-3841

Sonlight Productions Youth Ministry was formed in 1980 by a group of youth ministers to meet the needs of Black teens and young adults. Its initial purpose was to develop youth and young adult Black Christian leadership by ministering to their spiritual and social needs in the context of an inter-faith fellowship. *Sonlight* uses the mediums of music, drama, media, and "rap studies" to accomplish its goal.

One of the mainstays of the *Sonlight Ministry* is its "Midnight Special." Held every other month, the "Midnight Special" gathers young people from across the city into an intense and supervised 5-hour variety program centered around a special theme. It is a most effective "youth experience in the Lord." A program for any given evening (usually on Friday night) will include "the Hotline" (a community devotional); music (contemporary, by dedicated Christians in the Black experience); drama (for example, short skits and plays); "rap studies" (discussion oriented biblical teaching related to issues relevant to Black youth and young adults); relationship-building activities; counseling; and refreshments.

At any given "Midnight Special" between 200-300 participants and staff will attend the meeting, seeking to learn more about the Lord Jesus. Many non-Christians come to find the Lord as a result of this ministry. They are attracted by its contemporary and creatively fresh approach. Also, many believers have been strengthened through this ministry and have sought to reproduce this kind of youth program at their local Church.

In addition to its "Midnight Special," *Sonlight Productions Youth Ministry* offers weekly Bible studies with a discipleship emphasis; the "Son Players" (a drama troupe) and "Son Sound" (a music ensemble with band) groups that make hospital, prison, public housing development, and Church visitations; "Son Power," a monthly newsletter; seasonal ministries including "Sonlight," the Chicagoland Christian Youth Conference (August, 1986), "Candlelight Dinner Playhouse," and its Easter production.

Sonlight Production Youth Ministry is a youth program that is alive and well. It carries out its program with a high degree of success and is the kind of program to which a congregation can look with assurance to supplement the Christian education of its young adults.

2. Christian Education Enrichment Center
1439 W. 103rd St.
Chicago, IL 60643
Directors: Rev. John & Cleophas Sanders
(312) 233-4499

The *Christian Education Enrichment Center* is one facet of the ministry of Urban Outreach. It was developed for the purpose of promoting excellence in urban Christian education among members of local congregations.

The *Enrichment Center* has a good library of biblical, Christian education, and Black history reference books, a visual aid center, an audio-visual department, a Christian education tape library, and a Leadership Training component offering seminars three times a year. In addition, the *Christian Education Enrichment Center* is open and available for use during weekdays and Saturdays. The *Center* also publishes a quarterly newsletter providing insights into Christian education and information about other resources.

Local churches can make good use of the *Christian Education Enrichment Center* for purposes of training its young adults. It is a prime site for improving the study skills of students, a place where they can learn to study with a hands-on approach. Just the young adult's exposure to available literary resources is worth a tour of the *Center*.

Some of the classes offered during the Leadership Training seminars are: "Old Testament Survey," "New Testament Survey," "Understanding Teaching," "How to Study the Bible," "Black People in Biblical History," "Principles of Discipleship," "Understanding Teaching," "What the Cults Believe," "The Gospel of John," etc. A variety of instructors from different backgrounds are engaged to teach these courses. The curriculum is being broadened to include other subjects, and the information disseminated is pitched for the average Church member. Young adults can profit much from this teaching ministry.

Each first Saturday the *Center* has a *Lesson Illumination* and *Teacher Enrichment* class. And each third Saturday it holds a *Sunday School Superintendents Seminar*. Particularly those young adults who are in leadership training can make the most of these class sessions.

The *Christian Education Enrichment Center* is a pioneering work of Black Christians. The success it has enjoyed during its brief history points ahead to many profitable years ministering in the area of Christian education among Blacks.

3. National Black Christian Students Conference

(Correspondence)
Post Office Box 4311
Chicago, IL 60680
Co-Founder/Chairperson: Ruth Lewis Bentley, Ph.D.
(312) 722-0236

The *National Black Christian Students Conference* was organized in 1973 for the purpose of ministering to Black Christian college students on white campuses. It was organized as an exclusively Black conference with the focus of ministry being the Black community. Since the time of its inception the focus of *N.B.C.S.C.* has grown to include those Blacks who are college or graduate students on both Black and white campuses, as well as other Black persons from the community who are concerned with the wholistic liberation of Black people.

The purpose of *N.B.C.S.C.* is *1) To challenge Blacks students to a deeper relationship with and understand of Jesus Christ as Lord and Liberator;* and *2) To call Black students to commitment to the Black community by struggling for our wholistic liberation. One of the organization's aims is to call students to a commitment to the Black community in terms of location, finances, time, and resources.*

Any congregation which senses that its college students may be slipping away from the Church may find assistance in *N.B.C.S.C.* The organization "speaks the language" of Black college students and challenges them to become committed Christians and servants of their Church and people.

The *Conference* convenes in Chicago each November for three full days of intensive dialog and teaching, centered around a spiritually and socially relevant theme. The last few years the theme has been "Bridging the Gap Between the Academy and the Streets." The students were challenged to explore ways and means how they as Christians can bridge the gap between the "haves" and the "have-nots" within the Black community.

The program for any given *N.B.C.S.C.* gathering will include: community building exercises, Black history instruction, challenging messages, devotional studies, indepth strategy sessions, family worship, cultural activities, a "Black Agape Festival" (banquet), and much more. Previous conferences have dealt with such subjects as the Black Church, the Black Family, Leadership in the Black community, etc.

N.B.C.S.C. also publishes its own literature. One of its best sellers is its: *Handbook for Black Christian Students: How to Remain Sane and Grow in a White College Setting.* Many people have found this book most useful for helping their students cope with difficult educational situations and dynamics so that they preserve their resourcefulness for the Lord and the community. Also, over a 13 year history *N.B.C.S.C.* has accumulated a sizable resource bank of tapes and "position papers" covering most any topic relevant to Black people from a Christian perspective.

The *National Black Christian Students Conference* is presently a one-of-a-kind organization. We know of no other organization of its kind or caliber. It has much to contribute to the development of a Church's young adults, and to the furtherance of bringing the claims of Christ to bear on the experiences of Black Americans.

112

Summary and Conclusion

The Maturation of Emerging Black Young Adults — An Ongoing Challenge

Summary

Throughout this work we have touched on various topics related to understanding, reaching and teaching Black young adults. In our first part, *understanding Black young adults*, we identified Black young adults on the basis of their age range, their emergence, and nine signs of their maturity. We also profiled Black young adults in order to better get a feel of their experiences. Then we proceeded to give a definition of "emergent Black Christian young adulthood" — a discussion of our concept for the development of an exemplary Black Christian young adult.

In the second part of our study we turned our attention toward *reaching Black young adults.* Black congregations were encouraged to start working with the young adults they already have, and begin nurturing them in a group setting. We then touched on staying in contact with college students, evangelizing the unsaved, especially Black males, restoring the backsliders, and exercising watchcare over college students who are away from home. One good idea for reaching Black young adults is to be found in the area of developing interest centers for the idle unemployed, a program whose merits beg to be tested.

The final portion of the book covered the topic of *teaching Black young adults.* In this section we formulated our definition of emergent Black Christian young adulthood into an objective with five aims, covering a Church's ministry to its young adults. Assuming that most of a Church's teaching for young adults would occur during the Sunday School hour, we provided an explanation of an aim for teaching young adults and the model of a teaching plan that can work in this setting with this age group.

Next we provided a "test of emergent Black young adulthood," to be used as a guide for the development of the young person who is changing into a young adult. And then we covered how young adult leaders can empower and equip young adults to strengthen the Church through the use of spiritual gifts. Finally, we gave brief synopses of three Black Christian organizations which are working in the area of Christianly educating Black young adults: *Sonlight Productions Youth Ministry; the Christian Education Enrichment Center;* and *the National Black Christian Students Conference.*

Conclusion

Throughout this work we have sought to communicate the idea that the group we know as young adults are **an emergent class of persons.** They are emerging from adolescence and are emerging into early adulthood. They are emerging economically, psychologically, socially, accountability-wise, emotionally, axiologically, community-wise, and volitionally. Further, the Christians of this group are emerging spiritually. That is, they are "coming into their own in the Lord."

Our burden in this work has been to instruct and persuade leaders of young adults that an effective young adult ministry is essential for improving the quality of the Black Church and the life of Black Americans on into the 21st century. It is the young adults who will either make the Church or break her through their own broken lives. *If Black Christian education does not give itself to overseeing the spiritual/social maturation of Christian Black young adults, it will have failed its Church, its people, and its Lord, Christ Jesus.*

Furthering the emergence of Black Christian young adults is an ongoing process. There are other areas impacting this educational process which still stand to be further explored, developed and put to good use. Time nor space did not allow us to pursue, for example, the role Christian Black young adults

114

have in the institutional development of the Black community. Neither did it permit us to fully discuss leadership development for Black young adults. Also, we desired but were not able to provide some additional biblical examples of spiritually motivated and ethnically conscious young adults. And a section on musically using the Black spirituals as an educational and motivational medium could have been enlightening.

Be that as it may, we trust that what has been written on these pages will keep the ball rolling for those who sense the calling of God to become involved in reaching and teaching Black young adults. Our Black young adults need their leaders. Let us not forsake them. Let us say to them as David said to Solomon: *"Be strong, and show yourself a man, and keep the charge of the Lord your God"* (1 Kings 2:2b-3a, RSV).

Appendix

The Holy Spirit and Christian Spirituality

Not everyone talking about "spirituality" these days is talking about the same thing.

The term may be used in reference to the non-physical realities of life, with no particular emphasis on its goodness or its badness. (Demons are *spiritual!*) When others speak or sing of spirituality they are talking about something more or less rooted in personal moods and feelings as one relates to being more "religious." Others would take us back into the cultural ethos and collective consciousness of our ancestors, that we may be in accord with their spirits. Along with these and other dimensions of what is called "spirituality," some people have such personal conceptions of spirituality that only they themselves know what they mean and strive to attain!

Within the midst of confusion and a growing diversity of opinion and experience of spirituality, the Christian, who also speaks of "spirituality," must carve a place for a Christian position and understanding. Hence, we speak of "Christian spirituality." To be sure, among Christian circles there are varied understandings of what it actually means to be spiritual. Yet, we believe there is ground for a common definition to which most Christian persons can adhere.

Is the work of understanding spirituality as difficult a task as many of us are lead to think based on the wide differences of popular beliefs and opinions? Not if the subject is approached from a concrete (!) basis. Briefly, let's lay a foundation for a common understanding of spirituality.

First, we speak of "Christian spirituality" because for us it is *Christian.*" Simply the spirituality we speak of is centered in Jesus Christ, for He is the center of the Christian faith. And since Jesus' work of redemption, through His atoning death on the cross and His actual resurrection from the dead, was the center of His work on earth, so ought the spirituality of Christians be guided by a purpose in accord with this work.

This means that Christian spirituality is centered in Jesus and has a purpose related to the redemption of humanity. As Jesus said, "The Spirit of the Lord is upon me, because he has anointed me to preach good news to the poor. He has sent me to proclaim release to the captives and recovering of sight to the blind, to set at liberty those who are oppressed, to proclaim the acceptable year of the Lord" (Luke 4:18-19, RSV).

Second, the data (content) which provides the bases for and informs Christian spirituality is the Bible. For the Bible is the bases for our understanding Jesus and his redemptive work, the center of Christian spirituality. So when we want to understand what it means for a Christian to be spiritual, then we must read and study, not popular opinions, not the humanistic works of "enlightened" men and women, not astrological information, not religious syncretism - not anything but the Bible.

For certain, the Christian ought to "read" and study life itself, as well as the writings of credible persons to ascertain their thinking and to learn those things which are obviously accurate and true. But when it comes to the matter of understanding and being spiritual, the Christian is obligated by His relationship to Christ to study and live by the Scripture, and to judge all other information based on the truth which the Scripture teaches. As the Apostle Paul said, "If any one thinks that he is...spiritual, he should acknowledge that what I am writing to you is a command of the Lord" (1 Corinthians 14:37).

Third, Christian spirituality is produced by the Holy Spirit whom Jesus has sent to the Church from His Father. Christian spirituality is centered in a person, the third person of the Godhead Who has centered His own work in Jesus: the Holy Spirit (John 14:26; 16:13). Since the Holy Spirit is a gift sent by God to each Christian, then each Christian has the potential, and ought to strive, to be spiritual through His presence. "For all who are led by the Spirit of God are sons of God. For...you have received the spirit of sonship. When we cry, 'Abba! Father!' it is the Spirit himself bearing witness with our spirit that we are children of God" (Romans 8:14-16, RSV).

It is the true belief of those who are professed Christians that the only genuine Christian spirituality is that which is produced by God the Holy Spirit. Without the presence and work of the Holy Spirit there is no spirituality which can be said to be "Christian" or acceptable before God.

Fourth, Christian spirituality produces holiness in the life. The spirituality of Christians is not without the essence of godliness which is holiness. Where there is genuine Christian spirituality there is a manifest holiness in the life.

One passage of Scripture which shows this clear relationship is 1 Thessalonians 4:1-8. When teaching these Christians what it meant for them to be in "sanctification" and "holiness" in contrast to being in sexual immorality and passionate lust, the Apostle Paul told them: "For God did not call us to be impure, but to live a holy life. Therefore, he who rejects this instruction does not reject man but God, who gives you his Holy Spirit" (7-8, NIV).

Christian holiness should pervade all aspects of living and human relationships: family life, time management, business dealings, personal recreation, political work, community activism, etc. But there is perhaps no other area of our lives which evidences the holy working of God than in our human sexuality. This is especially apropos since we live in a rampant sexually permissive society.

When we speak of Christian spirituality in this regard there is no place for homosexuality, bi-sexuality, uni-sexuality, pornography and general impurity, adultery, fornication, incest and the like. There is no place for the expressions and relations of sexual intercourse except between man and wife within the God instituted context of heterosexual marriage. Then there is plenty of room for sexual enjoyment and fulfillment. For within God's will he sanctifies and blesses the sexual relations of a man and his wife (Hebrews 13:4; cf. 1 Timothy 4:3-4).

Based on what has been said, then, what is a good working

definition of Christian spirituality?

Christian spirituality, as biblically based and defined, is that sacred character and conduct of a Christian whose life and way of living is under the dominating control of the Spirit of God Who energizes him in ways accordant with Jesus' work of redemption.

(Black Christian Spirituality, © 1985, Rev. Walter Arthur McCray, Black Light Fellowship.)

Publications may be ordered from:

Black Light Fellowship
Post Office Box 5369
Chicago, IL 60680
(312) 722-1441

Office:
2859 W. Wilcox
Chicago, IL 60612

(Include postage and handling.)
(Bookstores and groups may order direct; at a 40% discount, payable in advance.)

Copies may also be purchased directly from:

Urban Ministries, Inc.
1439 W. 103rd Street
Chicago, IL 60643
(312) 233-4499